WHAT'S NEXT?

SPORTS   **LIFE**   BUSINESS

TO:
Anna

Thanks for the support!!
Keep Striving, keep pushing, keep praying!!
Attack Life!! God Bless!!

D. J.

VFL
Go Vols!!

WHAT'S NEXT?

SPORTS   **LIFE**   BUSINESS

HOW TO
TRANSITION
LIKE A
CHAMPION

DERRICK FURLOW, JR.

Inside photos provided by the author.

Author photo and cover graphics provided by 360 MediaGroup.
Page layout by Win-Win Words LLC.

**Readers of this book are also encouraged to purchase the
companion curriculum workbook, *Sports Life Business:
The Transition PlayBook,* available at retail outlets,
amazon.com, and www.sportslifebusiness.com.**

Sports Life Business (SLB) and Impact, Inspire & Empower (IIE) are
registered by the author.

ISBN: 978-0-9992746-0-6

Printed in the United States of America

To my mom, Lisa Wyatt, thanks for giving me life,
figuring it out, and never settling.

CONTENTS

ACKNOWLEDGMENTS

FIRST OFF, I'D LIKE TO THANK MY LORD AND SAVIOR JESUS CHRIST for giving me life, the stage, and the purpose to Impact Inspire & Empower people and for letting this book be used as a tool for the kingdom.

Then I have to thank my beautiful wife, Amanda, for believing enough in me and my purpose to allow me to quit my job and pursue my purpose in life! I'm forever grateful to have you by my side.

I'd also like to thank my parents, Lisa Wyatt and Derrick Furlow Sr., for bringing me into this world. Even more importantly, I thank my mom for the lessons that turned into blessings that she taught me as a single mother raising me, my older sister Nickey, and younger brother Roman.

I want to say thank you to step-parents Leonard and Delores for treating me like their own. And to the rest of my siblings Mesha, Micah, Tiffany, and Aisha—I love y'all.

I'd like to thank my grandparents, Grammy (Elizabeth), Grandma Mary, and Grandpops (Aaron) especially for telling me, "If you stand up straight, nobody can ride your back."

I want to thank my team, Chris Walden and Cassy Hayes, for their help, endless support, and for believing in me since day one of SLB.

I want to thank everyone who has ever mentored me and helped me become the person I am today.

Last, I want to thank the game of sports, football especially, and the life lessons it has taught me.

SPORTS   LIFE   BUSINESS

SLB PREGAME

W E ALL FACE CHALLENGES, MANY OF US DAILY. To work through these issues, we strive to follow life principles that we have either learned on our own by surviving hard knocks or had taught to us by someone wiser than us. This is what *What's Next?* is all about. This book is aimed primarily at college and professional athletes who have left their sport or are contemplating doing so, and are open to advice and direction from someone who has been in their shoes (or cleats)—me. Perhaps you seek guidance on what to do with the rest of your life and career beyond football, basketball, baseball, or whatever your chosen sport is. I can provide answers and guidance. In this role, I'd like to think that I am the "been there, done that" guy who can help you navigate forward as you move beyond this pivotal point in your life. My goal is to impact, inspire, and empower you to achieve and succeed as you follow along the path in front of you.

When you are making a major change that has you facing a new direction with many unknowns (and at times much trepidation), you want to reduce your learning curve and give yourself a quicker path to success. You want to stay a step or two ahead of the crowd. You can do this by applying the **right** lessons and principles to everything you do from this moment forward. This is true whether it's sports, life, or business—they all apply.

Through this book I will reveal the principles and winning-edge fundamentals I have learned, observed, and used in sports, life, and business. I'm passing them along with the hope you will internalize and implement them to give yourself what a sports fan or commentator might call an "unfair advantage" in your own arena of sports, life, and/or business. By "unfair," I don't mean doing anything illegal or sinister or that involves cheating or underhandedness. I'm using the phrase "unfair advantage" in this context to imply that you can achieve the kind of tremendous success that draws profound admiration from others. Maybe you can even leave them awestruck as to how you accomplished so much in such a short amount of time, while doing it the **right** way.

As you go through your journey encountering whatever **odds** or obstacles might pop up, remember **ODDS (Others Don't Determine Success),** you do. I'm going to share with you game-changing principles I learned, many of them the hard way and a few without warning. By reading this book, you can learn these life principles in advance of needing them. Take the time to study and practice these philosophies; just like in sports, practicing these principles daily will give you a winning edge. You can get to where you want to be if you apply them consistently.

We make our biggest mistakes in sports, life, or business when we fail to apply the positive principles and lessons we have learned from other areas of our life. We sometimes jump into an endeavor with the expectation that we will experience a flawless outcome, making minimal mistakes along the way. Somewhere in there, though, we neglect to utilize the knowledge we have acquired; we do things without thinking them through. We fail to take the time to recall principles that could have helped us. We are supposed to learn from our mistakes—not forget them and forge ahead recklessly. Most of us forget about these success principles or lessons because we don't take the time to reflect on them, to go over them in our head pondering how they could benefit us long after we've learned them, then apply them to the new frontiers of our existence, such as going into business after playing football.

My hope and expectation is that you will take away some intangibles about sports, life, and business that, when used correctly, will create the tangible outcomes you want in sports, in life, and in business. There will be no more excuses after you finish reading *What's Next?* No longer will you be able to say, "I didn't think about that," or "I didn't know what to do." No more excuses. Regardless what circumstances you encounter at any given moment, you will have at your ready recall memories and lessons learned from something you have endured, experienced, heard about, or read that you can apply to help you achieve your desired outcome. These principles and lessons will help propel you uphill. Here's a truism that applies to sports, life, and business: **"You can't go uphill with downhill habits."**

Before I reveal the principles of uphill habits to you, starting in chapter 1, I need to tell you about a common obstacle that can derail people in sports, life, or business. It's one of the worst possible things that can happen to you, and it can be devastating to your future if you don't have a plan in place (one that I'm about to give you). This obstacle I'm talking about is an insidious disease, one that is more common than the common cold and which can spread faster than the most aggressive cancer.

This affliction has snuffed out more lives than any disease known to man. It's been around since the existence of the human race. For centuries, it went undiagnosed . . . until now. It can't be treated with medication, a change in nutrition, or with extra exercise; therefore, doctors can't help. Neither can parents. In fact, they, too, might be afflicted, and most likely they passed it down to you at birth. This disease could claim your life, too, unless you decide to fight it—smartly.

You might be asking yourself, "What is this disease, and how do I fight it before it does me in?" You might even be wondering if you have already contracted the disease. **In layman's terms, it is known as Living Below Your Potential (LBYP).**

First, don't panic. Start with a self-diagnosis. Ask yourself, "Am I where I want to be in life right now?" If you answered yes, the good news is that you don't suffer from LBYP. If you answered no, then ask yourself this: "Have I done everything I could do today to help me get there?" If you answered yes to that second question, then you are suffering from stage 1 of LBYP.

Stage 1 of LBYP is not the end of the world; you're not **really** going to die from it. You still have time to do something about it. Just be grateful you caught it early. If, however, you answered no to both those questions, then you are in serious trouble. You are in stage 2 of LBYP. That's followed by stage 3, full-blown LBYP, which leads to the death of your dreams, your purpose, your passion, your pride, and your power.

Doctor's orders: you need to get to work, and fast!

SPORTS   LIFE   BUSINESS

1

WHO AM I?

I WAS BORN AT 6:09 A.M. ON SEPTEMBER 22, 1986, AT CRAWFORD LONG HOSPITAL in Atlanta, Georgia. I weighed in at six pounds, eleven ounces—the only problem was I came into the world not breathing; dead at birth. I had to be resuscitated, if you can call it that because, technically speaking, I wasn't even "suscitated" in the first place, at least not outside my mother's womb.

I must be here for a reason. I believe we all are; it's just up to us to make sure we find that reason and fulfill it.

There was nothing impressive about me or my life growing up. I was raised by a single mom and had two siblings, one older and one younger, which put me right in the middle. That put me in position to learn from my older sister's mistakes; on the other hand, I missed out on getting my way because I wasn't the baby. My dad was around, at least in the same area in which I lived, but he had his own family to look after. He was in my life but more so to provide for me financially than relationally; I did get to see him on most weekends

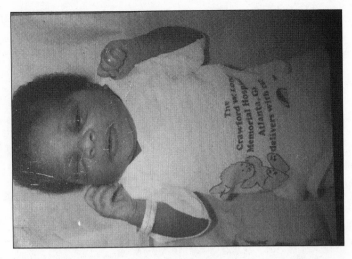

I came into the world not breathing, "dead" on arrival. But that wasn't in God's plans for me.

and when school was out. I always enjoyed those visits because it gave me a chance to see my other sisters. In addition to that, he always had more food as well as cable TV, which I did not have access to at home. I was too young to grasp it at the time, but having separate parental households provided a lot more than having just one. I would eventually get to experience having two parents in a home by the time I got to high school.

I spent the first half of my life (up to now, anyway) in southwest Atlanta; that's where I grew my roots. If you happen to know the area or have at least driven through or by there, maybe you can picture this: at one time or another I lived off almost every exit on I-285 South in and around the city, before we eventually moved to Griffin. All this moving around was by my mother Lisa's choice. In those days, I didn't really know what was going on. It would take me until I got into my twenties before I started figuring it out. I always wondered why we would move so much; as soon as I would get comfortable and settled in, and had made good friends, we would move. We averaged moving about every two years. I ended up attending three different elementary schools, and along the way I mastered the art of quickly making new friends. In the process, I also learned a few other critical lessons, even though I wasn't aware of it then. My mom was teaching me stuff even if she wasn't aware of it, although I'm guessing she was.

It was years later, while going back over my childhood in my head, when one of those early lessons became clear to me. This was in 2013, when I was home for Christmas and decided to ask Mom about all those moves. Before asking that question, though, I decided on Christmas Eve to revisit all the old apartment complexes in which we had lived while I was growing up in Atlanta.

One of the places was Overlook Atlanta, an apartment complex that had since been condemned. The apartment buildings were boarded up, and there were leaves and weeds scattered everywhere. My second stop was Deerfield, off Campbellton Road, which is run down. Lastly, I stopped at Stone Creek, also known as Tecali (I'm assuming they changed the name after its reputation got so bad that no one wanted to stay there).

As I headed out that day for my own personal "nostalgia tour," I had good memories of all these places, but that's all they were—memories. On my drive back through the area, looking around at all the places where we had lived, I felt thankful for having made it out of there. It was a reminder of the hand I had been dealt. There was one other place in which we had stayed for a while—government housing at Gilbert Garden, located off Cleveland Avenue. I didn't even bother going by there because it's just so disheartening to see my people living in those conditions. I recently found out that that housing had been condemned as well.

I'm grateful to be where I'm from and to have been brought up the way I was because I learned a lot. Growing up in a low-income environment surrounded by what we call "poverty" embedded in me a **FEAR** at a young age that this would be my life if I didn't make something of myself. It also made realize that if I don't achieve some sort of significance in life, I would not be able to come back and help others, for which I feel a moral **responsibility**. Those streets taught me street smarts in terms of surviving. It's only right that one day, when I've reached a **position** that I can pay it forward, that I do it.

After taking my trip down "Why Did We Move So Much" Lane, my eyes were opened. I thank God for my mom moving us like she did. We worked our way from the inner-city hoods of Atlanta to the outer-city suburb of Griffin, where I spent a good portion of my time. I didn't realize how bad it could have turned out for me if we had stayed in any one of those places longer than we did. That culture was all I had known, so it was normal for me—until after years of moving I found my "new normal."

You might have heard of a lot about these areas in rap songs. Some successful artists have come from these places. Hearing them mentioned in songs, however, doesn't make them glamorous, but merely the settings of success stories that are few and far between. Hopefully, those success stories are giving hope to people in those same situations. Being where you are might not be your fault, but staying there will be. If others can come from nothing to something and create their "new normal," you can, too.

Another vivid lesson I have continued to apply to my life is something from childhood that I remember as though it happened yesterday. It has been my building block for **discipline** since I learned it. Growing up, I was responsible for cleaning the bathroom or the kitchen, depending on which one was left to do after my older sister decided, after talking to Mom, which one she was going to clean. This one time, I was assigned to clean the bathroom. That was the chore I hated the most. The tub always had dirty rings around it, which meant I had to really get in there and scrub it to get it clean. Not to mention there was the need to clean up around the toilet, which I thought was about the worst thing imaginable. That's mostly my fault because my aim wasn't very good, and I just wanted to hurry and get it over with. My friends were outdoors playing football in a parking lot (we didn't have much grass), and I really wanted to be out there with them versus cleaning a toilet. So, I rushed through cleaning the bathroom, and then told my sister I was going outside.

As you might have guessed, this wasn't my typical look when told I had to clean the toilet.

I make it outside just in time for teams to get picked. Before I knew it, my mom was home, and she wasted no time making her presence abundantly clear to me. She came charging out to tell me to get back into the house and clean up. Of course, the first thing I said was, "I did clean up." I said this not knowing she had already gone behind me and checked out my work. Clearly, there was a

Football became my No. 1 sports-playing priority, but I also hooped it up for many years. Not sure about that T-shirt, though.

difference between Mom's definition of clean and mine.

As you might have guessed, I didn't play football that day. Instead I distinctly learned about the right way to clean, whether it was a bathroom or some other part of our home. Once I had cleaned the bathroom a second time, properly, Mom said, "If you are going to do it, do it right the first time" (and you would not have to do it again). This lesson taught me to never **cheat** myself, cheat the system, or cheat the process. This alone would impact the rest of my life in ways I would not ever expect.

Once I looked back at the bigger picture, I saw that my mom was teaching me things without my having to ask. Same thing when it came to our moving all those times. She was a single mom and wanted the best for her kids. Whatever the situation might have been, she was willing to get up and move to make it better. I took from that a commitment to never settle for where you are if it's not where you are supposed to be. I love and thank you, Mom, for that.

Where you're supposed to be and where you actually are, are usually two different locations. I found this out during my freshman year of high school. My mom was blessed to meet and marry my stepdad. It was a game changer for us after having lived in a family with three kids in a single-parent home, with Mom working at the Internal Revenue Service (IRS), which was a solid job. This marriage for my mom would bring another sister and two brothers into the household, bringing the total of parents and kids to eight. This was a new dynamic and interesting, and change came quickly. This time it was not my mom's doing.

My stepdad, Leonard, was an environmental engineer for Georgia Pacific at the time. His job transferred him, which meant we would have to move again. This time it was hundreds of miles away to Arkansas, which I couldn't even find on a map. Not only that, the news couldn't have come at a worse time for me. I had just started high school and was playing football and basketball, and running track, making a name for myself. Now I would have to do it all again, starting from scratch at a new high school in a different state.

This whole moving thing did not sit well with me at first. I fought it until one day, when I was visiting my dad and had a conversation with my stepmom, Delores. She talked about this concept of reinvention and how this might be an opportunity to go somewhere new and reinvent myself to become the person I really wanted to be. She said, "This could be your fresh start." That's when the light bulb went off in my head.

I wasn't really sure if she was saying this because she didn't want me moving in with them (which would've meant that I'd stay in the Atlanta area instead of moving with my mom and stepdad). That night, though, the more I thought about what she had said about "reinventing myself," the more it made sense and excited me. I thought about the name I was creating for myself in sports in just my freshman year in a state like Georgia, where there are great athletes everywhere. I figured I could dominate in a place like Arkansas. Prior to that moment, my having to move and not being in control of my life had left me angry and frustrated. This was the **motivation** I needed to take control of my life and my destiny, which is something I live by, still to this day. I wanted to make sure I got out of Arkansas as quickly as possible and return to Georgia as quickly as possible, and the only way out for me was through sports.

Sports, Life, Business Takeaways: Chapter 1

In this "Who Am I?" chapter, I touched on a series of early-in-life lessons that I hope you connected with in some way, with the realization that your circumstances most likely are different from mine. We all face our own challenges at a young age, well into our teen years. Note that each of the following chapters will also have an ending Takeaway section like this, asking you to write down some of your own thoughts relative to what you have just read in that chapter, applying the life lessons to your own life experiences and circumstances. While reviewing the lessons presented in this chapter and summarized below, take the time to think about what early lessons you have learned in sports, life, and business that could benefit you in other areas. Write them down and jot down a few notes about how you can use them now, using the space to write at the end of the Takeaways.

1. I believe growing up seeing poverty embedded in me a **FEAR** that this would be my life if I didn't make something of myself. **The fear of not reaching my potential was something I allowed to push me in sports to be the best I could be. Now that I'm an entrepreneur, it continues to push me daily to fulfill my purpose.**

2. This growing up surrounded by poverty also made me realize that if I didn't become significant in life, I wouldn't be in a position to come back and help pull up others; it's like this was

now my moral **responsibility. Feeling responsible to one day come back and make my home
city as well as this world a better place carries
so much weight for me; it is something I am
compelled to shoulder, and this has inspired
me to stay focused, both when I played football
and now as I continue my business pursuits. I
know people are depending on me to make a
difference that could impact their lives. I feel
some pride in taking on that responsibility, but
even more so I feel excitement, optimism, and
expectations that good things will come. I believe this.**

3. Those streets of Atlanta taught me street smarts,
including how to survive. It's only right that one
day when we're able to pay it forward, we do it.
**Positioning is key; you must be in position to
make your play. In sports, positioning is half
the battle; it means having players in the right
position to make the plays for the team to win.
I use this same philosophy in business as well.
You must put yourself in position to win so
you *can* win.**

4. Courtesy of my mom, my building block for **discipline is the truism that** "If you are going to do
it, do it right the first time." If you live by this,
you will not have to do it over. This lesson taught
me to never **cheat** myself, the system, or the
process. **The discipline of doing it right the
first time and not cheating myself came in**

handy during college. Being a student-athlete, following those lessons helped guide me to the high road and created outcomes I would not have achieved without them. Now it is my standard for performance in the world of business.

5. Never settle for less. **Never settling for less is second nature to me; it's the only way I could survive and grow. It's a lesson that's now embedded in my personality, and it has paid off for me in football as well as in the business world.**

6. Having to move and not being in control of my life when I was a high school freshman sparked an anger and frustration in me that ultimately ended up providing **motivation** for me to be in charge of my life and my destiny. **This motivation helped me realize that if I don't have a plan or direction for my life, someone else will. I had to put my foot down and get serious and focused about my life and setting goals, and that will never stop for me.**

Chapter 1 Notes

_____

_____

_____

_____

_____

_____

_____

_____

_____

_____

_____

_____

_____

_____

SPORTS   LIFE   BUSINESS

2

WHY ME?

M Y TIME WAS COMING AND I WAS ALMOST FREE. Living in Crossett, Arkansas, had felt like a prison sentence. I met some great people and created some great relationships, but that was not the place for me. The one consolation of being in Crossett was that I could focus on two things: getting good grades so I could play ball, and playing the best ball I could play so I could "get out of Arkansas" and head back to where I belonged. That's exactly what I did until ball got narrowed down to playing only football— no more basketball.

Football appeared to be the most realistic route out of Arkansas for my stepbrother Micah and me. Micah was a few months younger than me, but we were in the same grade facing the same challenge—not wanting to be in Arkansas. That's why we put so much work in on the field. We attended Crossett High School, and this would be our first year playing football together; in Georgia, we had gone to separate schools.

Our sophomore year was an adjustment for us, but it turned out OK. It became well known that we were the future of the team because of the high level of competition we had come from in Georgia. The caliber of football statewide changed for us, but it changed in our favor. I suppose we knew we had a step up on other teams. Knowing this, our mission in terms of what we wanted to get out of playing ball in Arkansas was to help our team win a state championship and grab the attention we needed to get a scholarship. That was our grand plan to get us the heck out of there.

During the off-season, Micah and I put in our work twice a day. We worked on ball skills on the turf and speed training on the track. For extra cardio, we would run to school at night versus driving just to get that extra work in. We were committed.

Apparently, what we had was contagious. Soon we had half the other guys on the team putting in the extra work along with us. They were working as if they had the same goals we did. I came to realize that it was going to take that type of **teamwork** during the season to produce the goals I wanted to reach; my goals were predicated on the success of the team's main goal, which was to win—a lot. I could see that my teammates wanted something more, but they were just lacking the confidence and the leadership needed to push them beyond where they had been pushed before, but now was their chance to do it. They fed off Micah and me, and our energy and **vision** for **winning**.

During those workouts, something shifted; true **friendships** emerged, and there was a teamwide buy-in to the hard work that would make winning possible. It begins with a belief in "me," the "me" being each guy on the team capturing that vision for himself. When you have dreams so big that it lifts up others around you to make it happen, it's something special.

Actions speak louder than words—you know that, right? As the next season approached, all the talk was about how our time is **now**, it's our time to win. Operation Get Out of Arkansas was in full effect—at least for Micah and me. The plan was simple: ball out, win state, and get the scholarships that would get us out of there.

Operation Get Out of Arkansas was in full effect— at least for Micah and me. The plan was simple: ball out, win state, and get the scholar- ships that would get us out of there.

Of course, things never go as planned. During the physicals that were required before we could participate in the first week of prac- tice, my brother got the news that due to his growth spurt, he had a small bone missing in his lower lumbar; this meant he could not be physically cleared to play football that year, or possibly ever, depending on how well his back healed. His only other practical option, and the one he chose, was to tough it out, wear a back brace, and see how the bone grew in over the next six to seven months. If it grew fast enough, he might be able to get back to playing football, maybe even this year and before the end of the sea- son. Talk about a game changer! It was for him as well as for our plans and possibly his entire life. All that hard work he had put in during the off-season would have to be put on hold, but Micah was determined to not let it be in vain. It would take that same level of work he had sweated through over the off-season to get him through this so that he could overcome this roadblock. This became part of our mission, his circumstance giving me at least the extra fuel I needed to drive us during the season. Now it was on me and the rest of

The short and the long of it. I wanted to change the game, but the game changed me.

the boys to execute the plan we had talked about all off-season, and we would have to do it while missing a key ingredient in Micah. If we did it right and won enough games, I knew he could possibly make it back during the playoffs.

The season started and we were quickly rolling, rattling off win, after win, after win. We had some close calls and we played some tough teams, but the purpose we were playing for was so big that the **adversity** we faced did not derail us. Before we knew it, we were one game away from finishing the season undefeated and starting our championship run. We were winning, and I was balling and creating the attention I needed to get my scholarship. Meanwhile, my brother Micah was a doctor's appointment away from being told if he could rejoin the team and play the remainder of the season.

As good as things were going, would you expect anything

less than good news? Of course not. Micah was able to return and play, rejoining the team as we entered the first round of the playoffs. Everything had come together, and now it was time to finish the deal. If only it was that easy. We played a tough team in the first round of the playoffs, but we walked away with the victory. The second game was a fight to the finish, but we pulled it out. Now we were one game away from playing in the state-championship game, and I could taste victory, not just for our season but also for the great plans I had for my life. All along it had been like a script—a movie screenplay—and I had written it. To now see it playing out gave me the confidence and belief that whatever I put my mind to was possible.

Too bad that feeling didn't last long. We lost our next game, which was a state semifinal, meaning there would be no state championship for us that year. After all the work, we were all back at square one. I could **taste** success and now it was gone, and all I saw was failure since we had come up short. Great things had come from the season, but it was not enough for me. I had achieved small goals, I balled and I got attention, but we didn't win state, which was the stamp on the season I needed to achieve what I was looking for. The only way I could look at it was, we had more work to do. Being so close and coming up short would end up pushing me more than I could ever have imagined. Luckily that was just our junior year; we still had one more year to complete our mission, so we immediately got back to work after the season.

Often, we find ourselves asking, "Why me?" That was the question I kept asking myself after waking up from knee surgery in Monroe, Louisiana. I had torn a meniscus weeks before starting my senior year of high school. When I woke up,

I was further **blindsided** when I heard the news that the doctors had repaired not only my meniscus but also my anterior cruciate ligament (ACL). The injury had been even worse than initially diagnosed.

Thoughts raced through my head after hearing this news: *From finishing one game short of a shot at the state championship and helping to put our school in Crossett, Arkansas, (and me) on the map, I am now out for the season. I am irrelevant on the football landscape, and the chances of my ever getting a scholarship and playing football in college are now in question, big time. Why me?*

"Why, God?" were the first words out of my mouth. I was devastated. I had big dreams of playing college football on the highest level in the Southeastern Conference (SEC), preferably for my home state of Georgia as a "Bull Dawg" (as in University of Georgia Bulldog). This would get me out of Arkansas and back into Georgia, killing two birds with one stone. If I couldn't make this happen, I would consider myself a **failure**. Not just because I was letting myself down, but because of all my teammates who had supported the mission and put in extra work for me, the people rooting for me to win, and the people who were depending on me to succeed so they would see evidence of hard work pay off and inspire them to chase their dreams. I was not sure what was in store for me at this point, but I knew it had to be something big. I had come too far to **quit and let my journey end like this**.

On the drive home from the hospital, I'm not sure what it was that came over me, but I became more determined than ever to play in the SEC, regardless of what it took. I felt this setback was like my test to see how bad I wanted it. How **committed** was I to achieving the goal of playing football in an SEC school on the Division I level? As crazy as it

Top photo: I'm looking for running room. Bottom photo: Me (No. 14, on right) and my boy Michael Williams probably discussing whether I keep the ball or hand it off the next time Coach calls a reverse.

sounds, I was convinced that's where I belonged, and I would get there despite having only nine months to make it happen. My mind was made up; I'd play in the SEC at the University of Georgia. My journey through rehab would be the number-one determining factor in considering major programs. Time was of the essence. Players typically enrolled during the summer to get ahead on classes, grades, and learn the college playbook, all of which gave me a shorter window to recover.

Recovery from an ACL injury is usually a year—I had nine months, and not only was my **dream** depending on me, it felt like my LIFE was depending on me. The "Why me?" question would get answered, but, in reality, the most relevant question I could have asked is, "Why not me?" The answer I got from that second question surprised me. Not only did it surprise me, it confirmed me, energized me, validated me, and gave me hope for the future! I came to learn that football was the stage on which God was allowing me to do his work, and I had not been using it properly for him. It was all about me and my selfish goals and dreams—me, me, me and my, my, my (as you probably already surmised by reading this far). It had been all about my ambitions and my goals for my life, not his. He needed to get my attention and **humble** me, and God's mission in that regard was accomplished. He had to take football away so I would **focus** on him. This allowed me to realize that what I had been through, and the tasks at hand and ahead, were not about me; they were far bigger than me.

God showed me that my past battles, trials, and tribulations had shaped me, molded me, and equipped me for my current situation and my future celebrations. He just wanted me to be **dependent** on him and not on football to make it happen. This newfound understanding and dependence on God was a victory in my eyes, even though it didn't look like it from the outside, and I certainly wasn't feeling it at first. "Every victory begins a new race." I was ready. "I **trust** God enough to do whatever he wants me to do."

I felt he wanted me to be the example. I know you might be thinking, "Be that example for whom exactly?" Let that "whomever" go through their own **adversity** themselves. Well, being that example could mean being the inspiration for a friend who might be battling something similar or even worse than a knee injury; maybe they needed to see a model of perseverance or how to endure the ups and downs ahead of them. Maybe it's a family member about to get diagnosed with a life-threatening disease, and he or she will come to think that life can't go on or that all their dreams will never be accomplished. Or it could be a coworker on the verge of divorce who needs to see an example of what fighting for what you love looks like. Perhaps it could be a complete stranger or someone you've never met who hears your story, and it gives them that extra jolt of hope they need to make it through. In my case, I had to be the one who set the new standard for my family, to create the new normal for perseverance, and to prove that there are no excuses for settling for less. My mom did not settle, doing all the moving we did to get us in a better situation, and neither would I just because I was injured. I had no excuse to settle.

One thing about the community of Crossett, and I'm sure this is typical for a lot of small communities around America, people never really leave the area. It's like, once you're there, you are there for life. Some of the people I had gotten to know were OK with that, but the ones who hung around me wanted more out of life. I believed that by working through my setback and coming back, I could show them that you can make a way out of a journey that looks like a dead end. I wanted to show them that it could be done, regardless of the circumstances. No one who came after me and knew of my comeback would have an excuse for not making it out—if they really wanted to. It was at that moment that I knew that everything would be all right if I just went to work and trusted in the Lord, even if it meant taking the path least traveled, just as long as the destination was the same.

Why me? I now know the answer: no one else in my sphere of influence was battle-tested; they hadn't been where I'd been and emerged! No one was prepared like I was, in this exact moment, to face this task and be the example. If not me, then who? What if I had asked that same question, "Why me?" but God had decided to let someone else take my place as that example, only for them to fail while taking my spot in history—maybe they lose the battle and don't get to live the rest of their life telling the story of triumph? So that victory speech never gets shared because it doesn't exist, and now everyone else who was supposed to learn from that, who should have been destined to be impacted, inspired, and empowered, never hears the story—**my** story! Now their life will forever be changed, and there'd be no way of knowing what my story would have done to change their lives and its trajectory. Then it would all be my responsibility. That's the "Why me?" in all this. Are you ready to bear the burden? Most people are not. Don't be one of those people, complaining about their circumstances. Be the one who used his or her circumstances as a means to victory, and pass that hope on to others!

Sports, Life, Business Takeaways: Chapter 2

While reviewing the lessons presented in this chapter and summarized below, take the time to think about what early lessons, similar to the ones here, that you have learned in sports, life, and business that could benefit you in other areas. Write them down and jot down a few notes about how you can use them now, using the space at the end of the Takeaways to write.

1. It became well known at our new high school in Arkansas that we (my brother Micah and me) were the football team's future based on the level of **competition** we had experienced in Georgia. **Competition was something that made me better in sports, especially when competing with those I felt had more talent than me in some areas. This understanding pushed me to be better in sports but also in life and business. In life, I realize I don't have to compete with anyone in particular; internally, though, it forces me to compete to give myself the best life compared to where I was or am. In business, competition pushes you up or out until you decide to dominate your space. By learning this early, I was conditioned years in advance to be an entrepreneur. Entrepreneurship is something that involves a competitive or dominative nature, and by competing in sports so long, this felt second nature to me.**

2. I soon understood it was going to take **team-work** during the season to reach the goals I wanted to reach. I couldn't do it alone. **In my sport, there were eleven guys for one team on the field, meaning everyone had to do his part and play his role. We believed in "Together everyone achieves more." This became my outlook on life: it's crucial whether you are on a football team or raising a family together; whether you're a father, a single mother, or even the kid. Everyone has a role, and when done right, everyone wins as a family. This team concept for business has been instrumental and has changed my life. I love the feel of team in business because it allows each individual to stay in his or her own lane, do what he or she does best, execute, and win. And when individuals who make up the team win, the whole team wins.**

3. During the time I was in high school in Arkansas, I could see that my teammates wanted more, but they lacked the **confidence** and **leadership** needed to push them to go get it. This was their chance—who knew what life had to offer in little Crossett, Arkansas, beyond high school? **This skill of leadership was something I knew I had in me, but I had never been in a situation where I had to lead. I came to realize it was a situation of, "If I don't do this, it will not happen." The mission we were on forced that out**

of me, which was a blessing. My teammates saw something in me that I didn't see in myself, and they knew I saw something in them that they didn't see.

4. The purpose we were playing for—a state championship in football—was so big that the **adversity** we faced did not derail us. **The toughest but most valuable lessons come through adversity. My sports career showed that if your WHY is big enough, the HOW won't matter. My knee injury jeopardized my collegiate career.** At the same time, it taught me that anything can happen in life and business as well when you're on your way to the top, but ultimately, it's not what happens to you that counts, it's how you respond to it. This gave me a tough skin moving forward. Not that I expected endlessly smooth sailing for the rest of my life, but I now realized that when things get tough or go wrong in life or business, I have an edge because I have handled adversity before. All I have to do is focus on the WHY I have to make it through, and then HOW I make it through handles itself.

5. Weeks before starting my senior year of high school, I was **blindsided** by the news that the doctors had had to repair not only my meniscus but also my ACL. **This was a lesson for me to learn how to cherish what I have, because it**

can be taken away at any moment. You never know what's going to happen, which is how I learned to maximize life. I know we don't know what tomorrow holds. When it comes to life and business, I now say to hope for the best but be prepared for the worst, and give every day all you got because you might not get another shot.

6. Until I injured my knee and had the surgery, my life was all about me and my selfish dreams, ambitions, and goals. It should have been about what God wanted for my life. He needed to get my attention and **humble** me. **I thought I was humble until my injury made me stop and take a recap of my life. I saw where it had been all about me and my selfishness. God showed me how he can give it and take it away if not used properly. I learned that my winning was no longer about me winning on my terms but about taking my own victorious story and somehow using it for the growth of his kingdom. The moment you lose track of that and think it's all because of you, you will have a problem. That lesson has kept me grounded, and I will forever give all glory to the Most High, my Lord and Savior Jesus Christ.**

7. There are times I would consider myself a **failure**. Not just because I was letting myself down, but because I was letting down all my teammates

who had supported the mission, the people rooting for me to win, and the people who were depending on me to succeed. **When you fail to achieve, it will impact more people than just yourself. That is a lesson I learned, which still to this day gives me that extra drive in life and business. The moment I fail to become the man I can be, it immediately affects me becoming the best husband and father I can be. In business, it is about becoming the best leader I can be and creating the best business I can possibly create. Done right, that legacy will live on long after me. I now know that failure in one area can affect everything and everyone around you; do not let it become a habit.**

Chapter 2 Notes

_____

_____

_____

_____

_____

_____

_____

_____

_____

_____

_____

_____

_____

_____

SPORTS   LIFE   BUSINESS

3

UNFAIR ADVANTAGE

I F YOU THINK ABOUT ALL THE SPORTS YOU HAVE EVER WATCHED OR COMPETED IN, you certainly have noticed how dominant players, teams, and organizations always have an advantage of sorts. In sports, we have something known as the "unfair advantage," which is always legal (we hope), and is that driving force that helps the eventual victor get the victory. When I was playing, the unfair advantage, once recognized, is what we would often use to create big plays in the game. It's what many people view as a mismatch. For example, it's having a linebacker come out of the box to cover the other team's fastest wide receiver in the slot position. If you have ever watched an NFL or college football game and wondered why the quarterback is always yelling out different words, signals, or calls, and having guys move around at the last second before the play, that's why. They are looking to create a mismatch also known as their unfair advantage. These mismatches often lead to explosive plays, and explosive plays can win or lose the game for you, depending on what side of the ball you are on. An explosive play is any play twenty yards or more. It's great for offense, terrible for defense.

So, you might be wondering, "What is the relevance of explosive plays in my life and in my business?" I'm glad you asked, but before I show you, let's think about Hall of Fame quarterback Peyton Manning for a bit. Manning is top two with Tom Brady among this century's quarterbacks, but Peyton arguably is the best quarterback to ever play the game. From his time at the University of Tennessee to his Super Bowl seasons with the Indianapolis Colts and Denver Broncos in the NFL, he single-handedly revolutionized the game when it came to calling audibles. An audible is designed to make changes in the play call or adjustments before the snap to create mismatches by running a different play, based off what the defense is showing. When executed correctly, explosive plays are made that normally change the game in his favor. Manning became notorious for his audible "Omaha."

Momentum is is one of those things in sports, in life, and in business that is hard to get but even harder to stop. The importance of finding your unfair advantage is so you can create explosive plays in your life and your business.

On any given Sunday, "Omaha" could have meant a million different things, or nothing at all. But the potential to produce an explosive play grabbed every team's attention on defense. Opposing teams would soon devise special defenses they would have ready just at those times to (hopefully) prevent the explosive plays. These explosive plays are critical to the game because they can help a team create momentum or take away an opponent's momentum. Momentum is one of those things in sports, in life, and in business that is hard to get but even harder to stop. **The importance of finding your unfair advantage is so you can create explosive plays in your life and your business.**

Based on all the events that took place early in my life, I would say that I often benefitted from an unfair advantage, or what most people might call having an edge. That's what I would like to call it, especially when it comes to **mental toughness.** I believe we all have unfair advantages, but they aren't created equal and most aren't used for advancement. In most cases, we end up using these unfair advantages as a crutch or to handicap ourselves. More people use them as excuses not to make it happen than as a rationale to make it happen. I was blessed to see the writing on the wall when it came to the presence of unfair advantages—I was able to recognize and maximize my unfair advantage; there are a few distinct ones that come to mind.

All the moving we did while I was growing up was never fun. That's why, as an adult now, I still hate moving so much. When I was a kid, we averaged a move about every two years. Right about the time I would get comfortable and find a new group of friends or a new best friend, we would again pick up and move. The more we moved, the more practice I got at making new friends. I learned how to make new friends faster and faster each time. I began to learn how to quickly read people, and in a matter of minutes I could tell if I wanted to be their friend or not. I was wrong a few times and people I had at first crossed off my mental list would grow on me, but for the most part I developed great people skills that worked.

Now that I'm older, we call this "people watching and networking." As a kid, we called it "making new friends." It took me years to realize that moving from one residence to another, something I despised so much as a kid, taught me some of the most valuable skills I need to succeed as an adult. The first is my ability to **adapt**. I learned to be comfortable with change in my environment, my circumstances, or whatever situations I would end up facing. The concept of never getting comfortable to the point where you are afraid to move forward toward something bigger and better—even if it's the unknown—is probably one of the most valuable lessons I took away from my childhood moving experiences. I'm not sure if my mom ever knew what we were moving to, but I do know beyond the shadow of a doubt that she knew wherever we were headed, it would be better than where we were.

As you might have noticed, I'm big on using phrases. One of my favorites is **"Make your next move, your best move."** Maybe that's ironic considering my childhood, but when I first started using it, I wasn't even thinking about our family's moves all over Atlanta. No matter, I believe it. Whether the conditions were good or bad during our moves, I also learned to keep my composure. That's another valuable lesson I've learned that I wouldn't trade for anything.

Getting back to the subject of quickly making new friends in new places, **likability** also is a big factor. It made it easy for me to be a new face and yet get along with everyone in the room, well at least most. I saw how important it was for my teammates to like me because of my **belief** that putting in the extra work and the **hard work** would pay off; if they did not like me, no way they could believe in me.

Likability also gives you a true advantage in life and business. To find a spouse, you must be likable (just in case you forgot). In the world of business, if people like you, they are willing to trust you. If they trust you, they are willing to listen to you. If they like you, trust you, and will listen to you, then they are most likely willing to do business with you. You might never need people for any of those things, but without likability, it won't happen anyway.

Each of these lessons has assisted me in different ways and in different areas, multiple times throughout my life, and I'm sure they will continue to as long as I live. Once you hear how my unfair advantage gives me an advantage in everything I do, maybe I will then be able to help you discover your unfair advantage and how to maximize it.

As I grew through those moments, there was another circumstance in sports that threw at me some of the toughest adversity I'd ever faced, but it ended up creating one of the biggest advantages I believe I have in life. I

Doubt takes you out of action, but action takes you out of doubt.

refer, again, to my knee injury while in high school. Once I tore my ACL and meniscus and was told I would miss my senior year of football, I felt a burning desire, passion, rage, or whatever you want to call it, to prove the world wrong. In part to make a point, I decided to work so hard in rehab that not only would I recover in time to make it to early enrollment as a football player at a college that next summer, I would also be back at full speed by our high school playoffs, and I would be playing. It was a long shot, but it's a belief I held firm to. I got to work with no time to waste.

OK, that brings me to another of my phrases: **"Doubt takes you out of action, but action takes you out of doubt."** So, I went to work. In rehab, I knew I was going to have to put in the extra work to get my knee back into football condition after my ACL surgery. It was here that I learned the true meaning of **hard work**. I thought I worked hard on the football field; I thought I worked hard in the weight room.

Even now I thought I worked hard in my business career, but my knee rehab in high school set the tone. It's a different type of working hard when you have muscles and ligaments that aren't ready or willing to do what you want them to do. In your head, you think you can bend your knee to a 180-degree angle, or you think you can leg press the weight with which you are used to warming up, but you find that you can't. That's a strange, frustrating feeling. I was having to really push myself to levels that normally would be easy for me. My leg could not handle more, even though my mind could. That was some of the hardest work to me, because I knew what I was capable of, but during the early stages of rehab those things weren't possible.

However, I did figure out a few things that gave me a sense of progress, but it was pure will. I was supposed to use crutches for three weeks; I used them for one day. That was a win. Then on day three of rehab, I talked my trainer into letting me get a machine to take home so I could increase my rehab sessions to twice a day. I figured that would cut the recovery time in half. We were rolling.

By day four, I was getting in two sessions a day between a trainer at the school and my own rehab work at home. My comeback wouldn't be denied. This was my test. This was God's way of seeing if I really wanted it as bad as I said I did. If it was to be, it was up to me, and I would have to earn every bit of it. God was not going to make it easy on me, but "If I put the work in, it was mine." That's how I felt, so I followed it up with massive action. I put in so much action that by day five, I had a slight setback. I was going so hard in rehab, I burst the staples out of my knee, and that led to an infection.

The infection hindered the process, but it did not stop the show. I continued to work, but now I had to pace myself,

During the recovery and rehab phase following my ACL surgery, I must've looked like this some of the time. I knew I was down, but not out.

dial it back a notch or two. But I never lost focus of my goal and desire to prove to the doctors and the sports world and **GOD** that if this was the example he wanted me to be, I was willing to work to make it happen. I would be back for my senior season regardless of popular belief.

That story did not end as well as you might have expected. We were missing too many key players, and the team did not make the playoffs. However, my goal of making it back onto the field and playing my senior football season became a reality. I made it back, even though they put me at wide receiver and made me wear my brace so I would not run the ball. I had made it back; I made it happen, drawing on that relentless mind-set and refusal to lose **attitude** . . . for not accepting the easy route and choosing to get to work like never before, pushing myself to and beyond limits I never knew I had.

Those three disadvantages that I learned to embrace early in sports and life are some of the most critical lessons I apply in every area of my life, especially in the business world every . . . single . . . day. Yes, that gives me an unfair advantage. In life, most people won't know your unfair advantage; in fact, half of us don't even know our own unfair advantage. It's crucial that you find yours. It could even be more than one thing that you believe gives you an advantage; but, again, first you must find it. Remember, your unfair advantage is whatever you believe gives you the winning edge, tangible or intangible.

These lessons I learned early were prepping me for the biggest challenge I had ever encountered post-knee surgery. I had decided to ignore all scholarship offers from college football programs that weren't Division I or in the SEC, even knowing that I had gotten only two serious looks from SEC schools **before** my injury. After my surgery, the University of Georgia had already moved on; my only other shot was the University of Arkansas—the Razorbacks, in whom I was not interested.

That's what happens when you think you have it all figured out as a teenager, and you burn all your bridges because you have all your eggs in one basket, as they say. That's what happened to me. The only good thing I learned from this is that when you burn your bridges, there isn't any turning back. In my case, I could not turn back because I had too much to gain and nothing to lose. I was now just a few months away from high school graduation, with no idea of what I was going to do.

One day I got home to find a letter in the mail from the University of Tennessee. They expressed interest in me as a student and invited me to the "Spring Fling," which was also the weekend of the spring football game. I saw this as an opportunity to really take a closer look at the University of Tennessee. Little did I know that the coaching staff had heard about me from some of my seven-on-seven games while they were recruiting stud receiver Ricardo Kemp out of Warren, Arkansas. I knew practically nothing about Tennessee; I had never really watched them, being that I was from Georgia, but, clearly, they were a blessing in disguise. I had seen Tennessee play only once and it happened to be in a game for control of the SEC East to see who would represented the East in the conference championship game in 2004; sure enough, Tennessee won.

There was something different I felt after I had been around those guys. I was not sure what love felt like, but if this was the feeling, it's safe to say I had fallen in love with Tennessee; it was like I was home.

God was up to something, knowing I would be on campus for that game. I wanted to meet the coaches and the players to see what Tennessee football was all about. Sure enough, I had a chance to speak with assistant coach Steve Caldwell, and I was invited over to the spring game which was the big scrimmage—the culmination of spring ball. I had never been to Tennessee before, but soon my mom and I found ourselves on the way to Knoxville, not knowing what to expect; again, the only thing I knew was that **God** was up to something.

When we got to Knoxville, I immediately had a chance to meet a lot of the guys on the team and get a feel for them.

I felt there was something different after I had been around those guys. I was not sure what love felt like, but if this was the feeling, it's safe to say I had fallen in **love** with Tennessee; it was like I was home. I had visited numerous schools, numerous campuses and camps, but none ever felt like Tennessee. From the moment I left the team, I knew this was where I was meant to be. It came time to go meet the coaching staff. At that point, my mom told me, "You got this," and I went off alone to meet the coaches. It was not like her to let me go on ahead by myself, and this told me she also knew there was something different about this place. Just a wild guess on my part.

Knowing my other SEC options were pretty much non-existent, all I was looking for was a shot going into this meeting. A shot to prove that I belonged in the SEC, repaired ACL and all. By the time the meeting concluded, that's exactly what they gave me—a shot, but at my own expense. They were not willing to take a risk on me because of my knee injury and surgery, until I could prove I was the player they had heard about and seen before. At this point, I was ready to prove to them (and myself) that I was better than the player they had heard about and seen before. So, we made a deal: I would get whatever aids, grants, loans I needed to get there, but as soon as I proved I was back healthwise, that football scholarship was mine.

Sports, Life, Business Takeaways: Chapter 3

While reviewing the lessons presented in this chapter and summarized below, take the time to think about what early lessons, similar to the ones here, you have learned in sports, life, and business that could benefit you in other areas. Write them down and jot down a few notes about how you can use them now, using the space to write at the end of the Takeaways.

1. My ability to **adapt** to our frequent moves when I was growing up helped me learn to be comfortable with change in my environment, my circumstances, or whatever situation I was facing. **This has allowed me to understand the ever-changing business world: I now know the most consistent thing in life is change, so I'm never going to allow myself to get comfortable. I'm always looking to get better, to move forward, making the next move for my family or my business our best move. Embracing change by being on the front end of it, or forcing change rather than reacting to change on the back end.**

2. My ability to meet people and make new friends quickly happened by default because of our moving around a lot. Now, my **likability** made it easy for me to be a new face but to also get along with almost everyone in the room. **I pride myself in being just one person away from**

knowing the world. I use those people skills daily to network. It's not what you know, it's who you know. You've heard that truism a thousand times, and it's been proven true at least a thousand times over. People like doing business with people they know, like, and trust. If they don't know you, they can't do business with you. Plus, "every business is a people business." Remember that.

3. I discovered the true meaning of **hard work.** I thought I had worked hard on the football field, and I thought I had worked hard in the weight room; I even thought I was working hard in my business career, but none of that competes too closely with my work rehabbing my knee. That set the standard. **I don't mind working hard to reach my goal. I believe we all want certain things, but only a few are willing to do whatever it takes to get them. It won't be easy, but that's part of God's test. It's designed for you to ask yourself, "How bad do you want it?" Most people don't want it bad enough; knowing that this is how it works in business allows me to believe that I will outwork anyone for what I feel belongs to me. I feel like I can't lose.**

4. Many of the events that took place early in my life, which felt unfortunate at the time, gave me an unfair advantage—an edge. At least that's

what I like to call it, especially when it came to **mental toughness.** For me, this came from having to move all the time growing up, because my mom said we had to. It came from my mom being a single mom, from injuring my knee in high school, from an assortment of other things that didn't go my way, or from pursuing goals not easy to attain. **It's been said, "What doesn't kill you, makes you stronger." In my case, it equipped me to be mentally stronger and prepared for whatever I would face in life or business. I didn't expect anything to be handed to me.**

5. I made it back from my knee injury. I made it happen (with God's help) through that relentless mind-set and refusal to lose **attitude** for not expecting it to be an easy route and for the willingness to work hard. That has given me one of my biggest advantages in life. **Half the battle is your attitude; it will either make you or break you. Your attitude will be what determines how you feel about a situation, which, in turn, determines how you act on it. It can either help take you to where you are looking to go or move you in the other direction—the wrong direction! You will never have the right situation with the wrong attitude.**

6. I fell in **love** with the University of Tennessee and Vols football; it was like I was home when

I visited there. I had visited numerous schools, campuses, and camps, but never Tennessee. But from the moment when I left the team—the players and I headed out to go meet the coaches—I knew this was where I was meant to be. **Love is when you know it's special, from the energy to the chemistry—you know that you have the right one (person to love) or are in the right place. That feeling of love is special, so I knew that GOD was up to something bigger than I could explain. Knowing that feeling of love and when something is right—not because you want it to be right but because it was meant to be—is still the qualifier I use today in life and in business.**

Chapter 3 Notes

_____

_____

_____

_____

_____

_____

_____

_____

_____

_____

_____

_____

_____

_____

SPORTS   LIFE   BUSINESS

4

SUDDEN CHANGE

S UDDEN CHANGE IS THE NAME OF THE GAME. THE PERSON WHO can create, handle, and respond to change the fastest usually comes out ahead of the person who doesn't make the quick adjustment. This common principle is often exemplified but never fully explained, so I'll do the honors. Sudden change is all around us, and it is expressed daily, but we are conditioned not to notice it unless it is in the form of an emergency. The success will come to those with the ability to create change, recognize it, adapt, and respond the quickest.

Surely you have experienced it in school with a pop quiz. You walk into class and take your seat as you wait to find out what lesson you will be covering today. Suddenly, the professor says, "Put everything away except for something to write with; we are having a pop quiz." You also experience it at home when you get married or divorced. It's common in the workplace if you are new to a job or if you get fired. Then there's the change of going from a full house to being empty nesters, or transitioning from having no kids to becoming parents. Sudden change is everywhere. One minute things are going one way and the next minute things are flying in the other direction.

I began my college football career carrying a chip, not on my shoulder but in my heart: "Don't carry the chip on your shoulder, people can knock it off; carry it in your heart," I once heard sports performance and motivation expert Tim Grover, author of *Relentless*, say. I was having to prove I was capable of playing Division I ball after my ACL and meniscus surgery. I turned down other scholarship opportunities for the one that felt like home in the SEC, at the University of Tennessee, at the price of being labeled "a preferred walk-on." In choosing Tennessee, even without a full football ride (yet), I had accepted the challenges that would come with that decision, not really knowing what I was getting into. My first UT summer camp came less than twelve months after surgery. I knew I had a lot to prove to earn **respect** from the coaches and the rest of the players, and to also earn my scholarship. All I could do was "focus on the gap between where I was and where I was aiming to go."

Coming in as a preferred walk-on, the expectations of what was expected from me as far as effort in practice, in meetings, in workout commitment, and in study hall seemed easier because of what I had already been through. Accepting the easy outs, which were available for guys not on scholarship, was not on my agenda. I acted the part of being a player on scholarship because I knew it was only a matter of time before I earned one, so I had to set the tone upfront. I attended workouts. I attended speed training. When it came to team runs, I made my times. I attended all the meetings (mandatory for scholarship guys). I put in the work with my boys before and extra after practice. I did exactly what was expected from the other defensive backs (DBs).

At the end of camp, I went to coaches Larry Slade and John Chavis and tried to make my case that I had performed as well as the other DBs during camp. I reminded them that this was my first full go after having had knee surgery less than a year earlier. The meeting did not go as I expected; the coaching staff denied my request for my scholarship. That was an eye opener; I was surprised but even more determined. I thought I had done what it took to earn my scholarship, but I walked away from that meeting knowing I would need to do more. I would need to crank it up yet another notch. Maybe I had jumped the gun in making my request even before the season had started. I am reminded of the maxim, "The work you did to get you there will not be the same work it takes to keep you there."(IIE: Impact, Inspire & Empower) I was prepared to go further, farther, harder, longer than any coach would ask of me; my rehab from knee surgery had gotten me to this point, and it had really trained my mind for **endurance**. Now I would have to take my game from merely fitting in to standing out to earn my scholarship. So that was my focus.

The work you did to get you there will not be the same work it takes to keep you there.

I knew my second chance would come around to prove myself in spring ball, and I couldn't wait. It **hurt** being denied the scholarship. No one likes being rejected, and this by far was the biggest rejection I had ever encountered. Maybe that's what I needed. This sparked a sudden change in me; it made that burning desire inside of me to accomplish my goal even hotter. That lesson in rejection made every other type of rejection I would face in life easy to handle, because I learned how to handle rejection. I had no choice. What did I learn, you might ask? I learned that you do not have to accept rejection. Most people just choose to; so I did not.

My first experience in learning the principle of sudden change arrived on September 9, 2006, in a game between the Vols and visiting Air Force. It turned out to be a close game that never should have been close. If we had executed to our abilities, it would have been a blowout. Instead, we found ourselves in a dogfight. As the game came down to the wire in the fourth quarter, there occurred a play that not only changed the tenor of the game, but instantly changed a young man's life; in fact, it nearly killed him.

The play that changed everything involved my teammate and fellow DB Inky Johnson. Inky, going full tilt, went to make a hit on an Air Force player streaking up the sideline. The result was a major collision that resulted in Inky going to the ground like a rag doll—he was out even before he hit the ground. Inky had made a monstrous hit, only it was the Air Force player getting to his feet, not Inky. He wasn't moving. Inky never got up from the spot on the turf under his own power. Soon, they were bringing out the gurney and loading an immobilized Inky onto it, to be carted off the field and taken straight to a hospital for emergency surgery.

This was the sort of sudden change in a person's life that puts him or her on an emotional roller coaster. Imagine the chaos that was going on in Inky's head. Doctors saved his life and Inky would eventually walk again—today he is a very successful inspirational speaker—but he lost all use of his right arm and would never be able to play football again. I remember going from mad because it was a close game that should never have been close, to being worried about Inky, to being excited we got out with a victory, to being anxious to get to the hospital to check on Inky. A lot of us were on emotional roller coasters that night. As they hauled him away across the field that night, none of us really knew the extent of Inky's injuries. Finally, after two days of not being able to check on him, we received permission to go visit Inky in the hospital. It was at this point that my life suddenly changed.

We all entered the hospital as a team unit; it was all the defensive backs and DB coach Larry Slade. I have never been big on hospitals in the first place, so I was very emotional seeing my teammate/brother lying in that hospital bed. There was nothing any of us could do to help him at that moment, except to support him and pray. As we stood there at Inky's bedside, I remember Coach Slade saying, "Inky, how ya feeling?" and Inky said, "I'm at peace." That statement hit me like a ton of bricks, and I realized I had been chasing the wrong thing again. Instead of chasing my dreams and goals to get this scholarship, I should have been chasing God. It suddenly gave me a new perspective on life, which I thought I had gained in high school after my knee injury. It also gave me a deeper level of **respect** for Inky. It made me see some of my own challenges in a new light; for which I am forever thankful to Inky. When I heard those words from Inky, I immediately said to myself, "How can I be so worried about my scholarship and playing time, while Inky is lying up here in a hospital bed saying he is at peace? I must be missing something, but whatever it is, I have to find it."

> *As we stood there at Inky's bedside, I remember Coach Slade saying, "Inky, how ya feeling?" and Inky said, "I'm at peace." That statement hit me like a ton of bricks, and I realized I had been chasing the wrong thing again. Instead of chasing my dreams and goals to get this scholarship, I should have been chasing God.*

49

As weeks passed, I continued to search for that peace Inky had mentioned. Sure enough, if you search, you will find it, and I found it. It was something I thought I had all along, but clearly it wasn't strong enough. It was my personal relationship with my Lord and Savior Jesus Christ. As I look back on life, I see how critical it is that we are in alignment with our assignment—not with ourselves, but with Jesus Christ. Most of the time we go through life not aligned with our assignment and wonder why we are not happy. We wonder why we struggle to make it happen, and we wonder why things are not working out according to our plans. I'm a believer that struggle comes from not moving in our assignment, which is God's will for our life. That's why I was not achieving the results I wanted in terms of getting my full scholarship.

If I was going to put myself in position to have **strength** like Inky in the midst of my trial (which I don't claim to be on the same level of Inky's trial, not even close), I had to get my life right. I have always heard that the Lord works in mysterious ways, and I agree. He let Inky's injury remind me that I was getting off track and needed to refocus on him. He was the reason I had made it this far, and he had the plan, I just needed to remember who was in charge. So that's what I did. I got locked into our Fellowship of Christian Athletes (FCA) chapter on campus and just let God work. This is when we began to make it cool to love the Lord through sports and not just in secret. Before too long, we had the whole team coming to FCA, because that's where everyone was on Monday nights.

At this point I could feel the Lord working on my spirit, letting me know that what I was going through spiritually was bigger than me. I believe he wanted me to be an example for my younger teammates as well as for those who were at FCA meetings but were still lost spiritually. One night during an FCA meeting, in front of the largest turnout we had ever had, I rededicated my life to serving him. God wanted me to make it public so that my teammates and other athletes could see the work he was about to perform in my life. I knew I had fought a good fight; I had finished my course; I had kept the faith (2 Timothy 4:7); the rest was up to him.

Learning to master the art of sudden change has been a pursuit of mine every day since Inky's injury. It has taught me to expect the unexpected, and, in the case of the unexpected, I have learned how to manage my emotions and focus on the task at hand—to not be distracted by worrying about what the outcome could be. This is a true test of **composure**.

Sudden change, in this instance, also played a major role in reshaping my perspective. Before Inky's injury on that collision play, my concern had been on almost losing a close game and not having the full-ride scholarship that I believed I had earned. The sudden change resulting from Inky's catastrophic injury helped me realize that things could always be worse. Regardless how bad your situation is, sudden change for the better is possible as long as you are willing to **fight** for it. Now, as I face any obstacle in life or business, I am prepared to attack it in a way that will push toward a favorable outcome. This is all because of what the game taught me about sudden change and the need to be grounded in my solid spiritual relationship.

The sudden change in my perspective was a change that became permanent. It allowed me to begin to see things differently after Inky's injury. As I grew spiritually in a way that empowered me, I also started to see my athletic and collegiate career in a different light as well. I got honest with myself and said, "Maybe my skills hadn't grown as much as they needed to make them want to offer me. I could now see the business behind college athletics and college in general, and that gave me a renewed **belief** that I could achieve what I was looking to achieve because I could now see it from a business perspective. The question I was now asking of myself: "What can I do to bring **value** to the team, the coaches, the program, and the University of Tennessee?"

I found the answer in that sudden shift of thinking. First, I needed the Tennessee football program for my scholarship, but I had never taken the time to ask what they needed from me, outside of my athletic skills, to want to give me a schol-

Even reporters watching our scrimmages were asking, "Who is that No. 6 kid; why isn't he playing more?"

arship. In this business deal, they were winning because they already had me at the University of Tennessee for free, so why should they give me a scholarship now? Why not spend that money to bring in more talent? I couldn't blame them if they were thinking this way. With my sudden change in perspective, I began to think like a businessman, putting myself in their shoes. Somewhere in there I learned that, outside of talent, it's always good to have athletes who are smart and can play multiple positions. This gives you more depth (helps the team), more athletes with good grade point averages (helps the team/coaches), and more athletes who are on course to graduate on time (helps the program). So, at this point I **focused** on giving them the **value** they needed to benefit them, and by default we both would win.

After realizing that my life wasn't about me anymore, my inner peace started to emerge. I didn't have to be a superstar; I just needed to make my plays. I needed to do what I do best and let God handle the rest. Every day I was focused on adding value to the team, coaches, and program. My saying was, "Make it so they can't deny you." That's what I did by becoming the best version of me I could be. It reflected in my grades by my having one of the highest GPAs on the team. In film study, I became a student of the game and could call the plays and checks—before a coach would ask—that should be made based on formations that opposing offenses were showing. In study hall, it showed because I went there to get work done, although it wasn't mandatory for me because my grades were good. And last, it showed on the practice field. Suddenly, coaches could not watch many plays without noticing my effort. They could overlook a lot of things live because there were always other things going on, on the field, but it's hard to overlook effort on film. It got to where reporters noticed me during scrimmages, and they would soon begin to question some of the coaches, "Who is that No. 6 kid; why isn't he playing more?"

We all know that once value exceeds cost, money is exchanged, and that is exactly what happened. It was to the point where the coaches had something to gain, as did I.

Now that I had their attention, my value was apparent on the field as well as in the classroom. We all know that once value exceeds cost, money is exchanged, and that is exactly what happened. It was to the point where the coaches had something to gain, as did I. Since I had not failed or dropped a course since summer or early enrollment, I had put myself in position to graduate in three years, which was a blessing from above. That value I had of graduating early would benefit the football program. So, two years into college, after everything I had gone through, the **dedication** prevailed. I got my full scholarship. To God be the glory.

Sports, Life, Business Takeaways: Chapter 4

While reviewing the lessons presented in this chapter and summarized below, take the time to think about what early lessons, similar to the ones here, that you have learned in sports, life, and business that could benefit you in other areas. Write them down and jot down a few notes about how you can use them now, using the space to write at the end of the Takeaways.

1. I went in knowing I had a lot to prove to earn **respect** from the coaches and to also earn my scholarship. **I knew the coaching staff wasn't going to give me a scholarship just because I thought I deserved it or because of who I was or because of my past. Since I was in a new place in my life, I would have to do new things to earn the respect that goes with being treated like a D1 athlete, which is exactly what I did. Not only did earning the respect of my coaches and teammates feel good, it validated me and gave me more confidence and allowed me to believe in my abilities. This lesson taught me that regardless at what level you make it to in sports, life, or business you must earn the respect of those on that level. Never expect them to just give it to you based on your track record; you must demonstrate the actions that make them want to respect you. By doing so, you will also validate to yourself**

that you belong and earned everything you strove for. This builds confidence that no one can steal from you.

2. If I was going to put myself in position to have **strength** like Inky's during my scholarship-seeking trial, I had to get my life right. **You are only as strong as your weakest muscle, and my spiritual muscle wasn't as strong as it needed to be. After seeing how strong Inky was during his adversity, I knew that if I could build up my spiritual muscle to become that strong, then nothing could shake me. The grind I was enduring to get my scholarship would feel like a cakewalk compared to any serious adversity that life or business could throw at me in the real world; things such as sickness, marital issues, financial issues, etc. This also taught me that no matter what I'm going through in sports, in life, or in business, someone else somewhere is going through something tougher; you might be the only example of strength they see, based on how you handled your situation. To this day, I strive to strengthen my muscles in every area so that regardless of how bad I feel I have it, I'm strong enough to be that example of strength for someone else, just like Inky was for me.**

3. What happened to Inky taught me how to expect the unexpected. In the case of the unexpected, it

further taught me how to manage my emotions and focus on the task in front of me—to not be distracted by what the outcome might be. That was a true test of **composure. This lesson has been a blessing to me in every aspect of my life. What I found out was that most people are unable to remain cool, calm, and collected when under pressure or in an emergency. Most people let the natural human response of fight or flight kick in; this compromises the ability to remain calm. This lesson served me for years in playing the game, especially when the team or I were not in the best situations to win or to make a play. Maintaining composure shows itself nonverbally; in return, it can model to your teammates how to remain calm and believe everything will work out. In the same way, I have been able to remain composed when making major life and business decisions or when I respond to major life or business decisions. The first major life and business decision that required oodles of composure and created sudden change was the decision I made on January 5, 2017. That was the day I decided to walk away from a six-figure corporate sales career after seven years at Wyndham to pursue a new goal of impacting, inspiring, and empowering people full time as an entrepreneur. The second major decision I made that necessitated composure was deciding to write this book and** accompanying curriculum. This wasn't just diving into the deep end of the pool; it was more like a cliff dive. But there I was, having never written a book or a curriculum before, now taking on the role of creating a program that would impact the way athletes transition after sports . . . while having my family and my livelihood riding on it. I take pride in being able to keep my composure and exercise sound mind in making the best choices for my family, my business partners, and me. I will work to make sure that never changes.

4. Sudden change helped me realize that things could always be worse; despite how bad your circumstance is, you must be willing to **fight** for what you want. I learned that people will fight only for things they believe are worth having. **Regardless for who or what you are fighting, if you want it bad enough, you must be willing to fight and die for it. Inky had put it all on the line to attain his dream of playing in the NFL. He did it to the extent that he almost lost his life. What he went through made it OK for me to fight for what I believed was right for me and to not back down from anyone or anything in making it happen, except God. God was on my side, however, so I wasn't worried about that. From that moment forward, I realized the ability to fight is what I would need in life and in business to make my dreams a**

reality. You must fight for most of the things you desire in life and in business—not just physically fight, but mentally, spiritually, and emotionally as well. The one who is willing to die fighting for what they want, usually gets what they want. At least that's so in the cases of Jesus Christ and Dr. Martin Luther King Jr.

5. What can I do to bring **value** to the team, the coaches, the program, and the University of Tennessee? That was the question I asked myself then. **I learned that this was the most rewarding question that I could have ever asked of myself. It paid off tenfold when I took my attention off what the scholarship would do for me and figured out what I could do for the program. It created a win-win situation for everyone. This lesson became significant when I entered life beyond college, when it came to networking and building relationships in the business world of sales and dealing with people. Everything comes back to the value-add proposition: What can you do for me? and What can I do for you? Once value outweighs cost, you get an exchange. This is exactly what I endured for my scholarship. By the time I got to the real world, I felt like I had a head start on my peers.**

6. Two years into college and after everything I had gone through, the **dedication** prevailed. I

got my full scholarship—to God be the glory. The grind paid off; it always does, just to what degree and how much is what you must determine. You have to be more committed to the outcome than the obstacle that is hindering you. I once learned that to DECIDE is to kill all doubt. Based on the root combining form of "-cide," which comes from the Latin term *cida* (meaning to kill), we end up with "homicide," which means to kill someone; "suicide" to kill yourself; and "pesticide" to kill insects. You must DECIDE that your mission will be attained. The time for completion might take longer than expected, but go at it head-on, and in due time the mission will be completed. This is a lesson I carry with me every day in life and in business. After completing my first major mission like that in college, I felt that I could complete any mission to which I dedicated myself. This one lesson has molded me and my mind-set into one that will do whatever it takes to succeed, once the decision has been made to achieve it.

Chapter 4 Notes

_____

_____

_____

_____

_____

_____

_____

_____

_____

_____

_____

_____

_____

_____

SPORTS   LIFE   BUSINESS

5

THE PLAYMAKER

A COACH TOLD ME LONG AGO "YOU'RE ONLY AS GOOD AS YOUR LAST PLAY." Meaning, do not rest on your past success. You might be doing a great job, but if you're in the game of sports, life, or business, you still must make the play, repeatedly. This is the outlook that drives me every day.

We've all seen stellar athletes we would describe as "playmakers." They are playmakers because they consistently perform at a high level. **Playmakers** never rest on past success. They are always doing, or at least looking to do, something to dictate or push the outcome of the game in their team's favor. Maybe it's the cornerback who times it just right to break up the crucial fourth-down pass, when another DB might have shied away from attempting the play out of fear of being called for pass interference. This is how all of us should be every day—striving to make plays. Be that playmaker in your sport, in your life, and in your business. Some people embrace this philosophy; most don't. If you do, you're already ahead of the pack—guaranteed.

Whether it's in sports, life, or business, you always want to be focused on making plays. All such plays, big or small, contribute to the desired outcome.

Let's break down the concept of "making plays." It's a sports term, but it is jargon that can be adapted to life and business. It's also a term common to most athletes' vocabulary. When it comes to sports, it's the person or team making the most plays—making things happen—that usually wins the game. Whether it's in sports, life, or business, you always want to be focused on making plays. All such plays, big or small, contribute to the desired outcome. Making the big play in business could be conceiving the innovative idea that produces a massive gain in incremental income when no one else could come up with an idea that hadn't been tried—and failed—before.

At the University of Tennessee, I was blessed to learn firsthand what being a true playmaker is all about; this was while playing with one of the biggest playmakers I had ever seen on any football field. Most know him as Eric Berry; we just call him "EB." From the moment EB arrived at Tennessee, everyone could see he was something special. Time after time in practice and in scrimmages, whenever someone was making a major play on defense, EB was either a part of it or the reason it occurred. Whenever there was a big hit, EB was usually the one making it. If it was a fumble, EB typically caused it. If there was a fumble recovery to be made or an interception to be picked, it often was EB getting his hands on the ball. It's like he was a magnet to the football. Somehow, he was always in position to make the play.

EB's the best example of a playmaker I have ever seen, and at this writing he was still making those game-changing plays in the NFL. A few of those game-changing plays, which happened to be some of my favorite plays performed by EB, came at my home team's expense (the Atlanta Falcons). In Week 13 of the 2016 NFL season, EB caught an interception and ran it back for a touchdown to give the Kansas City Chiefs the lead and momentum right before halftime. Apparently, that wasn't enough, though; with about 4:30 left in the game, with the Atlanta Falcons up by one but going for a two-point conversion to go ahead by three points, EB intercepted the two-point conversion pass and ran it back one hundred yards for a two-point play that gave the Chiefs the lead and, ultimately, the victory, 29–28.

In making so many plays, EB made the rest of us step up our game so it wouldn't seem like we had to depend on him (even though we did). He made making plays contagious. He sold me; I worked harder in the weight room, was much more focused at practice, and played better and with more intensity in games because of EB.

EB embodied the art of the playmaker on the field. He always put himself in position to make the play, and he always took advantage of the opportunity to make the play when presented with the opportunity. How did he get in position seemingly all the time? He knew his assignments inside-out and had great instincts—he was a student of the game. He learned the game, knew the tendencies, paid attention in film sessions, and applied all of it daily on the field. Most people think it was all because of his base athletic talent, but it was his hard work mixed with his talent that made him the phenom he still is today, playing in the National Football League. What he did rubbed off on me. What I learned from him was that I could take that playmaker's approach and apply it to every aspect of my life. So can you!

Not everyone is Eric Berry, but everyone can be a playmaker in his or her own right! That's me, No. 17, in the flow of the play.

Not everyone is Eric Berry, but everyone can be a playmaker in his or her own right! Ask yourself, "What is the biggest play I have ever made?" I am confident that after you finish reading this book, your next big play will be on its way. Have you ever thought about the success you have achieved so far; have you taken inventory, maybe even made a written record of the plays you have made—the successes you have achieved? I confess that I hadn't done this myself, until I got to this point in writing this book. A good time to start is now.

As I recapped the biggest achievements of my life, going over them in my head, I saw a pattern—a trend—that emerged. It was a trend of success that I had exemplified when it counted, and a lot of what I dug up in my head was stuff that had been buried for several years. I was cutting myself short, when I needed to be getting this stuff down because it's important to my career. If and when you interview for a job, it is vital that you have your "big plays" at ready recall to present when asked to talk about yourself. Sure, I'm talking about me here, but only for the purpose of planting a seed with you in terms of how you can apply it to your life.

Whenever my back was against the wall, or when I was down and people counted me out, or worse, there were times

I almost believed the naysayers and considered counting myself out somewhere along the way. Still, I'm pretty sure my actions never showed it. That was where the playmaker in me showed up. It wasn't my first, but it was definitely one of the biggest plays I ever made; eventually earning my football scholarship after my knee injury. Most of the time it felt like nothing was in my favor and everything was going against me—from not getting along with coaches, to not feeling appreciated for my efforts, to not getting playing time, to wanting to transfer and start over at a smaller school. It even included thoughts of quitting.

Whenever my back was against the wall, or when I was down and people counted me out, or worse, there were times I almost believed the naysayers and considered counting myself out somewhere along the way.

Then there was the time I signed my first arena football contract with the Knoxville Nighthawks of the Professional Indoor Football League. After two weeks of practice, head coach Chris MacKeown called me into his office to tell me they were releasing me. My heart sank. I had never been cut from a football team, certainly not as a professional. But before I accepted the terms and walked away, I convinced Coach MacKeown to give me another week; they didn't even have to pay me. If I didn't show up as the player they needed me to be, then I would release myself. Sure enough, that week turned into two weeks, and then I ended up starting eight games. Luckily that ability to make it happen before time had run out or before the opportunity had passed, had fueled me all my life, even though I hadn't realized it or even knew what it was.

In coming to this realization, I finally understood that I had tapped into that playmaker ability only in times where I

felt a real sense of urgency, emergency, or flat-out despera-
tion. I should have been acting on that throughout life. In
playing with EB at Tennessee, I had now acquired the confidence to make the play—to make things happen—whenever
I had to make it happen or simply decided to make it happen,
even if the circumstance was something other than what you
or I would call urgent. The question I asked myself—and
which I have answered—is, "How could I operate at that level
consistently, like EB did, and does, on the field?" That's when
I learned the art of being a playmaker. It's looking to be the
playmaker all the time, in my life and in my business, and
not just in sports—which is especially pertinent to me *now*
because I am no longer actively involved in sports, at least
not as a player.

I knew then, while still at Tennessee, that what Eric
Berry demonstrated on the field had rubbed off on me and
that my goal, then and there, was to be a consistent playmaker—not just in football. By then I knew my chances of
going to the NFL were slim to none. But I was a **playmaker**.
I immediately set out to apply that determined, focused
mind-set to school since I was in position to graduate
early—I had racked up plenty of credit hours. I wanted to
take advantage of being in that position to graduate early,
and not blow it. That was **Rule No. 1** that I had learned from
EB: Playmakers don't blow opportunities—and I was not
going to mess up this one.

Rule No. 2 was to **know** my stuff. I had listened to my
academic advisors and counselors, so I knew I was on pace
considering I hadn't failed or dropped any classes. Until then,
however, I had not really looked into how many hours I had
and exactly what classes (required and electives) I needed to
graduate, I just took their word since it was their job to keep

up with that stuff. I didn't know if these were easy classes or hard classes, or whether the classes I needed were even offered each semester—all the little academic things I had never cared to inquire about or research on my own. I was not being a playmaker, which requires taking responsibility for everything. I was missing some critical information, such as the fact that I was eighteen hours away from graduation. It turns out I could get it done in a reasonable amount of time, although the Western Civilization course I needed would be twice as long and twice as difficult unless I took it in the summer. Here's one reality about college, a human factor: in the summer, a lot of professors seemed more lenient and most classes are condensed to fit into a shorter term; so is the workload, which I found as a plus.

Getting my classes in order took care of **Rule No. 2**, which then advanced me to **Rule No. 3**: Put yourself in position to make plays. Learning about that Western Civilization class and the options of where it fit onto the school's academic calendar put me in position to make the play of graduating college early. Not only did I become the first person in my immediate family to graduate college, but I did it in three years.

Rule No. 4 is to make the play, which was to graduate a year early and have another year of eligibility left to still play football. EB wasn't there to put his hand on my shoulder and push me through this whole process; he didn't have to—he had already given me the push I needed, just by setting the example with what he did on the field. I was now on my way to being a consistent playmaker in every aspect of my life.

Applying these rules required me to be extremely focused because I was breaking new ground in my life, shifting a paradigm in how I did things, and it took some getting used to.

It was something new, and the attention to detail involved required a new level of **focus on my part**. If being a playmaker was easy, everybody would be doing it. Few do. Be one of the few!

To recap, here are the rules of the playmaker:

1. **Take advantage of the opportunity to make a play.**

2. **Know the game/know your stuff.**

3. **Put yourself in position to make the play via Rule 2.**

4. **Make the play.**

Those rules worked well for me in the classroom, so I figured I would apply them on the field, too. No, I did not turn into an EB clone; however, I did have my best year in terms of how I responded and performed in workouts, practice, film study, scrimmages, and games. If the rules of playmaking helped me improve, they can do the same for you. The improvements I made in my sales career at Wyndham Worldwide, which was my first and, as of now, my only corporate job after sports, did not happen overnight. I had to learn the sales game inside and out (Rule No. 2) to the point that I knew what clients would say before they said it. Doing so allowed me to become one of the top reps at that sales center. By default, that put me in position to make a bigger play and interview for a sales presenter's position that I wanted. Note, though, I was not the leading candidate for this position going into the interview because of some political stuff. But I'll bet on a playmaker over politics all day every day, because all I could do was focus on the rules of being a playmaker by executing (Rules 1–4).

Sad to say, I did not walk out of the interview with the presenter's position; however, they were shocked at my strong performance in the interview. Four weeks later, I was offered a fulltime presenter's position. Like I hinted earlier, I'll take process over politics all day. Learning new skills takes **patience**, which is difficult when you are focusing on being consistent and wanting to see quick improvement, but it's worth it.

The first thing I did was commit myself to Rule No. 1, in that I would take advantage of my opportunities to make plays. I am reminded of a prayer I said to myself before every game, every practice, and every scrimmage:

"Lord, let me play smart, play hard, play fast, and be relentless. Know my alignment and assignments, and make every play that comes my way, and make it so they can't deny me."

I prayed that prayer every year for many years, but at the time I had no clue of the ramifications it would have on my life once I was done playing football. But as I look back, I can see it was God putting me in alignment with my life's assignment, which was no longer football. Football was just a vehicle to take me though the course of completing school and to teach me the lessons about life I needed to learn. As I progressed through life, my prayer changed slightly, but it was uncanny how God laid it out for me. I began to ask God to lead the way, to put me in position to make the plays he wanted me to make, and to remind me to stay out of his way. As I reflect on it now, my prayer really didn't change. The only thing that was different was the stage on which I would make plays and the size of the crowd.

By making this commitment, I was now holding myself **accountable** for everything I did that had to do with football. Things I would normally allow to slide—which were small things such as finishing team runs or letting teammates off the hook for skipping reps—I no longer let slide. It was all about being consistent; that meant doing the small things right **every time**, from putting up the weights with the power Ts facing up to making sure there was no trash left on the floor in the locker room. Then I applied **Rule No. 2** to film study. Here, I could become as much a student of the game as I wanted. This would allow me to study offense and special teams. This was so once we got into a practice, a scrimmage, or a game, I would know like never before my opponents' tendencies, formations, checks, and possible plays. I took it to a different level. I did not become the best, but I learned enough so that, by default, **Rule No. 3** showed up in how I applied myself in practice, in scrimmages, and in games. I resolved to put myself in position to make plays as much as humanly possible. Once in position, it becomes a lot easier to execute **Rule No. 4**, which is to make plays.

I did not become a game changer on the field with these rules, but I was successful in learning to abide by them—I became a better player and a more accountable teammate. After that, I played in the most games I had ever played in my collegiate career, made the most tackles in that single season than all my other years combined, and received more respect from coaches in terms of being a ballplayer than I had ever received on any level. That respect alone was the ultimate compliment and validation acknowledging how far I had come on the football field. The rules of playmaking had allowed me to produce consistent results in college in the first two areas in which I applied them as a student and as an athlete.

Since it was working so well, I continued to test the "rules of the playmaker" and ended up going three for three in making major plays in college while applying the rules of the playmaker to my actions. The third and final play I made turned out to be something I had never imagined or planned, but it happened as the result of my following the playmaker rules. I ended up graduating from the University of Tennessee for the second time—two degrees in a total of four and a half years, this time with a master's degree in sports psychology while also playing my senior year—my fourth year—of college football. Being a playmaker became more than just something I wanted to be on the field; it was now what I was aiming for in life and in business. It was only right that I took the rules beyond the game.

Since leaving college, I have adhered to those same playmaking rules in my personal life and business career. I take the same approach and follow the same steps. Because of this, I am blessed enough to continue getting the same results "making plays." I believe these plays I am now making are nothing compared to the plays yet to come as I strive toward my potential, but I want to share them with you. In the moment of making these plays, they are essential to my confidence. Upon leaving college, I believed that I could play a game in life and in business that would be easier for me on the strength of how I had successfully applied the rules in a highly competitive environment. I knew then I could enter "the real world" and be able to apply the same principles that had brought me success to achieve more successes.

I played professional arena football for two years; started my own company; and helped consult, brand, and launch multiple companies. I even helped grow some companies that are experiencing success today. I helped bring awareness to, and raise close to twenty thousand dollars for, five different nonprofits in my first two years of philanthropy. I was able to assist a program that mentors inner-city youth. I also walked away from a full-time job on my original career track, ditching all that to go it alone full-time as an entrepreneur.

At the time, all those decisions seemed monumental to me, but over time they have shrunk into small things that needed to be done to fulfill my purpose and grow my dreams. I believe the same can happen for you wherever you happen to be, whether in the arena of sports, life, or business, provided you put the rules of the playmaker into daily practice.

Sports, Life, Business Takeaways: Chapter 5

While reviewing the lessons presented in this chapter and summarized below, take the time to think about what early lessons, similar to the ones here, you have learned in sports, life, and business that could benefit you in other areas. Write them down and jot down a few notes about how you can use them now, using the space to write at the end of the Takeaways.

1. The playmaker concept is why and how successful people perform at such high levels consistently. A **playmaker** never rests on his or her past success. They are always doing something to dictate or push the outcome of the game in their team's favor. **This lesson set the tone for the rest of my life. I take the time to celebrate any success I have in my personal life or business, but the celebration is always short-lived because I can no longer rest on my past success. There is always more to achieve, more success to taste, and more lives to impact. I've learned to build off the momentum of the last victory to help get my next one. You can do that, too. That's why it's important to keep making plays as long as you can. There will come a day when you can't make the same kinds of plays.**

2. Remember the rules:
   1. **Take advantage of the opportunity to make a play.**

2. Know the game/know your stuff.

3. Put yourself in position to make the play via Rule 2.

4. Make the play.

3. Applying these rules took extreme **focus** on my part. It didn't come easily for me. It was something new, and the attention to detail for the work I was putting in was new to me. It was a big step up the ladder of effort. It required a new level of **focus. Learning how to lock in with extreme focus has paid me back tenfold in life and in business. That's because once I got into the real world, I noticed that there are things thrown at us from every direction, and most people don't know how to manage or handle the unexpected and the unwanted. Through the game of football, where there is miniscule room for error, I learned how to apply focus by following the four rules of the playmaker. The game showed me how to apply focus. Once I entered the real world post-football, I already knew I needed to first identify and then focus on the most important task that would reap the most reward, versus majoring in the minor things (distractions) that life and business had to offer.**

4. It takes **patience** to learn new skills. **This is hard to do when you are also focused on being consistent. For me, the first time was definitely a learning process—I had no choice but**

to be patient. God knows it's a lesson I needed. It's a good lesson to carry in my pocket as I continue to face new challenges and new things that need to be learned. Patience is indispensable. Success can, and will, come your way if you exercise patience. Life and business are processes; quick fixes and immediate results are not the norm. Don't rush the process. Patience is a skill. You will have to learn how to use it when dealing with people, products, or services. I'm grateful I learned how to exercise patience early in life, yet I'm also smart enough to know that it involves an awareness and effort that must never end.

5. The first thing I did in abiding by the rules of the playmaker was to make a **commitment** to myself. I could not commit to anything until I could commit to myself. It all started by telling myself I was *all in*—no more searching for an out. Throughout my sports career, as well as in life and in business, I've gotten involved with numerous things but only committed to a few. No more. Anything I now commit to, I'm in it for the long haul. Whether rain, sleet, snow, I'm there. This means learning to say no to some things; spreading yourself too thin is a mistake. I learned that taking on another involvement and being truly committed to it is not something you see a lot of these days. It is

easy to be on to the next wife, next husband, next project, next dream, when you are not committed to yourself or not committed to the task at hand.

6. By making this commitment, I felt **accountable** for everything that had to do with the game of football. **The accountability factor alone was important for me to realize; if I could not hold myself accountable, how could I hold my teammates accountable? How about in life; how could I hold my future wife and kids accountable? As a businessman, how could I hold my partners and employees accountable if I didn't learn self-accountability? That one lesson would factor into a series of lessons, but first and foremost, it would start with me and my personal accountability to master the rules of the playmaker.**

Chapter 5 Notes

_____

_____

_____

_____

_____

_____

_____

_____

_____

_____

_____

_____

_____

_____

SPORTS　LIFE　BUSINESS

6
LIFE PREP

ONCE I STARTED TO REFLECT ON ALL THE SPORTS I HAD EVER PLAYED, especially football, I realized how fortunate I had been to be able to compete at one of the game's highest levels. I noticed it prepped me for life. Football is like the game of life, but in a controlled setting. You have pregame, which is what I consider and use for preparation of most of my "game-like" events in life, such as speaking and presenting. You have four quarters, which, for me, is often the gauge for my day, week, month, and year. This allows me to assess myself; where I'm at, where I'm going, if I am strong, and do I need to finish stronger.

Then, of course, there's halftime, except life doesn't stop. Halftime is just the time in-between anything that I'm doing when I can gather my thoughts and breathe, to see what's working and what's not working, so I can make adjustments.

Last, you can't forget that sometimes we have overtime. I just see it as going the extra mile and putting out the extra effort that it takes to compete and win at a high level; the same is required in the game of life. The game of football has quarters that are each fifteen minutes long; unfortunately, we don't know how long we have in the game of life, so it's imperative that we make every day count.

Both games have officials applying the rules and regulations along the way. Learn those rules and regulations, and keep an eye out for occasional yellow flags or blue lights. And the last correlation of them all is that each game has an objective and an opponent. Football's objective is to outscore the other team and win. Life's objective is to find and fulfill your purpose; by doing so you will win at life; in the game of life, the only opponent is you.

"Football is a lot like life." You hear that a lot as an athlete; it comes from your coaches; even your parents might say it. It's another sports cliché, but it's one that holds its weight, even though it's generically used and the correlation of how it's like life is often loosely communicated. It is often said, but is rarely shown. Most athletes hear it but are never taught how to make the correlation of their sport to life. It usually doesn't register until later in that athlete's life, if ever. **Communication** is vital in sports but also in life and in business; yet that ball—that message—often gets dropped. That's how **losing** in life and in business begins for athletes: they never get a clear message to make the correlation.

Through the grace of **GOD**, I was able to take notice and make that connection early in my life, at least before I was finished with college. Everything I studied, practiced, and was taught from the game I felt I could apply later in my life. Division I football in the Southeastern Conference is the biggest stage in college sports, despite what loyalists for the likes of the Big Ten, the Big 12, the Pac 12, and the Atlantic Coast Conference might counterclaim. Every day, even in the so-called off-season, we had practice of some sort related to helping us master our craft. This was so when the sun came up or the lights came on on Saturdays, we were prepared and had the confidence we could play flawlessly (even if we never actually did, but we came close a few times).

Before we talk about playing on the big stage, let me share with you some things I learned my senior year at the University of Tennessee—things I learned in football practice that I knew would prepare me for life. After three years of football camp, I finally decided to pay attention to the details of our camp schedule, instead of going through practices robotically, albeit enthusiastically. By really looking at the details of the schedule, I could see there was no wasted time. There was no white space on our calendar. We were always going from one thing to the next, doing something that would prepare us for the season ahead. Coach Lane Kiffin clearly understood the importance of priorities and time management—how to get the most out of us in the allotted time.

Through University of Tennessee football, I experienced the best time-management course possible in a university setting. The lessons that I learned from our camp's calendar comprised a million-dollar **skill** set. They displayed the importance of being efficient and maximizing the time you have to get a task done. It was a time-management class they did not offer in college. I saw that as a lesson that, when put to use, could help find that balance between being a student and an athlete. I believe I can say I had already done a good job of it. It also was a lesson for when I would get into the real world; it gave me confidence that I could get a lot of work completed if I just used my time wisely, like we did during football camp. It also gave me the insight that it's possible to

August 2009

Sunday	Monday	Tuesday	Wednesday	Thursday	Friday
2 • New Arrivals Report 9:00 am – 3:00 pm • 6:00 pm Evening Meal- 1st Time Participants	3 • ACA Orient. - New Arrivals • All Returnees Report by 2pm • Team Meeting: Administrative All • Team Meal 6:00	4 • Acclimatization Day 1 • 3 hours (Helmet Only) • 1 Hour (Walk Thru-No Equipment)	5 • Acclimatization Day 2 • 3 Hours (Helmet Only) • 1 Hour (Walk-Thru)	6 • Acclimatization Day 3 • 3 Hours (Helmet & Shoulder Pads) • 1 Hour (Walk-Thru) Summer Session II ends	7 • Acclimatization Day 4 • 3 Hours (Helmet & Shoulder Pads) • 1 Hour (Walk-Thru) *Welcome Back
9 OFF DAY –No Practice Meetings – no walk-thru 4:00 pm Media Day 7 pm Team Administrative	10 • Practice 6 & 7 • 5 Hours Total (Plus Walk-Thru)	11 • Practice 8 • 3 Hours Total (Plus Walk-Thru)	12 • Practice 9 & 10 • 5 Hours Total (Plus Walk-Thru)	13 • Practice 11 • 3 Hours Total (Plus Walk-Thru) • 12 Noon Off Campus Players Move Out	14 • Practice 12 & 13 • 5 Hours Total (P Walk-Thu)
16 FF DAY – No Practice 0 Social raining Walk-Ons port	17 • Practice 15 • 3 Hours Total (plus Walk-Thru)	18 • Practice 16 • 3 Hours Total (Plus Walk-Thru)	19 • OFF DAY – No Practice • Fall Semester Begins	20 • Practice 17 • 4 Hours Countable Activity	21 • Practice 18 • 4 Hours Coun Activity
24	25	26	27	28	

Our fall camp schedule at the University of Tennessee kept everybody pretty busy, and attendance was mandatory.

have a demanding schedule and still have time to have a life and raise a family and all the other things that came along with that—once that time came. I could see the lessons I was learning in the midst of going through football camp doing drills, even the ones that I **hated**; but I stayed engaged on a deeper level because I was learning more than just our football skills for the upcoming season; I was learning life skills for my upcoming life.

I remember one time getting our fall camp itinerary and, while flipping through it, I came across the page concerning possible disciplinary action as it related to the team's attendance policy. At first, I found it strange that there even needed to be a written attendance policy because—of course—I assumed

Wednesday August 5th

6:00 am	- Wake-Up
6:00 am	- Breakfast-Varsity Inn/Training Room Opens
6:30 am	- Freshman position meetings
7:00 am	- Position Meetings
7:30 am	- Walk-Thrus
	• Summer school -2nd session
8:30 am	- Coaches/Staff Meeting
9:00 am	- Strength & Conditioning Orientation (New Arrivals)
10:00 am	- Position Meetings-New Arrivals
11:30 am – 1:00 pm	- Lunch- Varsity Inn
12:00 pm	- Taping/Treatment
1:45 pm	- Position Meetings
2:45 pm	- On the Field
3:00 pm	- Practice # 2 (Helmet Only)
6:00 pm	- Dinner-Varsity Inn
7:30 pm	- Special Team Meetings
8:00 pm	- Team Meeting (Offense/Defense)
9:30 pm	- * Snack - Complex
10:00 pm	- Coaches/Staff Meeting
11:00 pm	Bed Check- Lights Out

Up at 6 a.m., lights out at 11 p.m. A day in the life of a college football player.

everyone knew he was expected to be at practice and go to class, as well as to be present for every tutorial, study hall, weight room session, training room session, and team meetings; all that is a given, right? How could any player in his right mind, having accepted a scholarship to a university, not know that already? But seeing all that written down just confirmed for me what was expected of us. Nothing was left to chance in terms of knowing the outcome, or the consequences, if we failed to abide by the rules.

Expectations are key to **winning** or **losing**. The coaching staff made sure their expectations were clearly **communicated** so that everyone was on the same page. It set the tone for camp, even for those guys who had been through camp before; they needed to know what was expected of them in this camp.

That lesson of communication and accountability is one I firmly hold on to today as a follower of Jesus Christ as well as a leader, husband, and someday father. One day I will have to set the tone, and I can't assume or expect everyone will just somehow know it. There must be a standard set because there are always consequences for things we do or don't do. There must be guidelines we live by and lead by; seeing the attendance policy in camp was what set the tone for me.

One day I will have to set the tone, and I can't assume or expect everyone will just somehow know it. There must be a standard set because there are always consequences for things we do or don't do.

Then there were the practices themselves, where you go from getting **knocked down** to getting up—or where you can go from being a hero to a zero—in a matter of seconds. This is where I began to break down how we went through every conceivable game situation throughout the week. Coach was getting us prepared for the unexpected so that it would not be unexpected. Let's take it to another level. Can you possibly imagine a daily "life practice" in which you go through every conceivable situation that life could throw at you so "if" it ever happened, you would be prepared to face it? I didn't think like that until that moment.

Nowadays, when I look back at football practice, or "life prep" as I like to call it, I can see how anyone who has played sports or even followed a sport super closely, can work to achieve the **winning** edge in life and business as well. My sport was football, but you can take any sport that can be practiced in a controlled setting, and through that sport you can learn lessons that give you a competitive edge—that includes virtues such as discipline and work ethic—in life and business. In football, we were allowed day in and day out to practice to ensure we would get it right under the lights on game days regardless what play was called or what situation popped up. It was in those moments that I could see how I was also being prepared for life and a post-football business career. It was an experience that I believed gave me an edge for life after football, and it's an edge that you current athletes have or anyone who has left the sports arena has and can use to your advantage.

Here's the thing, though: You don't get a chance to practice at life or business. You have no timeouts available when parental duties call. You can't throw a yellow flag when a competitor gets a head start on you. You can't just stop and say, "Hold on, I need a water break," in the middle of a presentation pitching your new product. There are no substitutions for someone to take your place in life or business; if there are, you might not ever get your spot back. There's pressure and no easy ways out. All you can do is make **adjustments** and roll with it, just like you would have to do in the game with the clock running and the score being kept. If you don't make the adjustments and learn to roll with it, the next person is waiting to come along and outwork you for your spot—just like in a team sport, where there is always a second- or third-stringer right behind you knocking on the door. When this registered with me in school, football practice wasn't practice anymore. It took on a whole new meaning; it gave me a renewed energy and sharper focus because I saw it differently. It used to be practice; now I call it Life Prep 101.

At the time, I would no longer call it "practice" because I realized it was giving my teammates and me a crash course in looking beyond football to see how life and business worked. Each day while practicing football—and this includes playing in the games—I got to develop my attitude for how I would respond or react to life and business decisions based on what was put in front of me (or thrown at me) on the football field. Think about that for just a second; that cuts deep. Think about anything you have ever done that required practice or some sort of extended preparation; certainly, you realize now that everything you have practiced has produced for you an outcome, whether good or bad, favorable or unfavorable. You get to **choose** your attitude, action, and approach the next time you are presented with this same scenario in practice.

Isn't this the exact same thing with life? We do something, we get an outcome (good, bad, or indifferent), and then we choose how we react or respond. Then, however we decide to respond, this will then produce another outcome, hopefully one that is in your favor. Those daily reps in football are molding us and shaping us for the next game as well as for what will come next in life, and over time and through repetition our responses and reactions become like muscle memory; they are ingrained in our mental and emotional DNA. If we learn these lessons properly, they don't become something that just comes and goes—they **stick** with us. Once you learn them, they can go on forever, holding you up in life and business, but you must learn them in the first place. What's said is that most athletes never learn how to parlay these lessons learned in such a way as to benefit from them outside the game of sports. This is your chance to rise above the others! Practice hard and seek out the lessons of life and business that will profit you later.

I had all this time to master how I would react or respond to anything I had ever practiced. Now you can see why I no longer call it practice, and why I call it Life Prep 101. The key ingredients to life prep are the habits that we create daily—the good ones, the bad ones, the ugly ones, and the ones that we do not know we are creating. What life prep taught me was that my habits that were created in practice would carry over into the game, from the game over into life, and from life into business. I had to get them right and seize the opportunity. It really registered why coaches had us watching film every day so we could see our mistakes, successes, and, most importantly, our habits. It's crazy to practice bad habits and believe you will get good results. Practice does not make perfect, perfect practice makes perfect. So, if you're practicing bad habits and wondering why you're not getting the desired results, you might want to do a self-evaluation—a "film session"—on yourself just like you did playing the game. You will get a chance to see your habits. From there you will know what you need to do is to change your habits. From there you will know a changed habit will create a changed outcome. These were the types of lessons life prep was teaching me.

Practice does not make perfect, perfect practice makes perfect. So, if you're practicing bad habits and wondering why you're not getting the desired results, you might want to do a self-evaluation—a "film session"—on yourself just like you did playing the game.

Life prep will repeatedly show that the person with the best habits will consistently produce the best results or desired outcomes. Half of the problems we face today are related to the fact that people don't know or recognize "life prep lessons," which are opportunities to learn and get better. *"The chains of habit are too light to be felt until they are too heavy to be broken."* – Warren Buffett

As I grew wiser on the practice field, I realized that life prep wasn't just about going *through* the motions; it was more about learning *from* the motions. We can learn from everything we experience. Like Coach Trooper Taylor always said, "Every moment is a learning moment; either you are getting better or you are getting worse. You never stay the same." That's the type of attitude you need to develop in life prep. Once the day is finished, and real life has kicked in, you will have to look at yourself in the mirror and hold yourself accountable to God, your family, yourself, and whoever else might be depending on you. Then you must ask yourself, "Did I get better or worse today?" Did I move closer to my dreams or further away; if I did move closer, how so? If I didn't, why not? What can I do right now to make today count?"

This is the shift you make when life prep is at its finest. Of course, this stage of life prep hits different people at different times—in life or business. That's why I wrote this book, to give you a head start and a heads up. Regardless of when life prep hits you, it's about being **coachable**; the key is to embrace it when it does hit you and move forward with it. If you are **not coachable**, you will fail to embrace life prep and will be one of those people who moan, groan, and complain, and will settle and become content with whatever life or business has thrown at them. They will remain static and eventually move backward as life passes them by. Life prep is presented in many ways and will have many ways of teaching you once you are aware of it. What I learned is, *"When the student is ready, the teacher will appear."* (Proverb). Ask yourself, "How much life prep have I been missing out on?" Most of us only begin to notice once the lessons become expensive.

During training, it's called **recovery time**: how long it takes for you to recover your oxygen and energy between sprints or sets (lifting weights). Recovery time is a good judge of what kind of shape you're in. When I was playing football, I saw it not only as how long it took for me to catch my breath from working out or running, but also how long it took for me to get up once I was **knocked down**. Ask yourself, "How long does it take for me to bounce back from defeat in business?" How long do the tears last, how long does the disappointment last, how long does the heartbreak last when cheated on or after a divorce? How long does hopelessness last when hardship hits?

Learning about **recovery time** was great during strength and conditioning, but it must be taken beyond the game and applied to your life and your work. I knew if I could have a short **recovery time** on the field or in the weight room, I could figure out how to carry it over into life or business. We always hear about people working on their physical cardio; when was the last time you heard someone working on their mental cardio? That's the mental conditioning that sports teach you, and I learned it in football. I believe it's important to remember, "Where the mind goes, the body follows." That's what I felt I needed, and that's what I took to heart: taking that mental cardio from the game and applying it to life and business.

To get ahead in sports, in life, or in business, I would

need a faster recovery time physically and mentally; that's one of the great dividers in sports. I figured it had to be the dividing line marking the separation of people who are just getting by from the people who are thriving in life and business! Think about it; have you ever been at the gym working out and seen the person who does an exercise for thirty seconds and then rests for five minutes before starting the next exercise? They stay in the gym two hours for a workout they could have completed in forty-five minutes if their recovery time was what it should be. Then, you see a maniac (in a good way) in the gym who is all over the weight room, gets his work done, and is out of there before you know it. He takes little if any break between workout sets. He has an incredible recovery time. That's the type of physical and mental recovery time we must have to succeed in life and business!

Sports, Life, Business Takeaways: Chapter 6

While reviewing the lessons presented in this chapter and summarized below, take the time to think about what early lessons, like the ones here, that you have learned in life that could benefit you in other areas. Write them down and jot down a few notes about how you can use them now, using the space to write at the end of the Takeaways.

1. In practices, you can go from getting **knocked down** to getting up, or go from being a hero to a zero in a matter of seconds. **The best lesson I learned from this is that it's just a part of life. The same thing was going to happen in every aspect of my life, so why not learn to handle and adjust to those feelings and emotions now? This is so once it happened later, I would be prepared to handle it well because I had been there before and had felt that before.**

2. Anyone playing sports or following the game super closely can get the **winning** edge in life and business. **This helped me realize that it wasn't just about winning on the field; it was about winning off the field as well. I wanted to win in sports, in life, and in business. To do so, I would have to ramp up my game in life and in business to the level I had ramped it up on the field. With my football career winding down, I realized I needed to find a way to**

carry it over into life and business so I would not feel as if I had to start over once I was done with the game. Here is where most athletes and people miss the connection. I'm grateful I didn't miss it, but I'm determined to pass along to others what I learned along the way so that others, like you, can make that connection.

3. **Communication** is vital in sports but also in life and in business. Often, though, this is where the ball is dropped. **Losing** in life and in business begins for athletes when they never get a clear message to make the correlation. **I believe you win some and you lose some, but losing does not have to be a permanent thing if you learn from it. I would rather learn from winning than from losing, but if you lose, it is critical that you learn from it so that you do not repeat it. Many athletes end up losing after they leave the game because they never go back and assess their earlier wins or losses so they can learn from them. They reminisce on the good times and bad times, but they fail to take with them those things that could prevent them from losing in life and in business, now that the game is over for them.**

4. The lessons that I learned from our camp calendars comprised a million-dollar **skill** set because they displayed the importance of being efficient

and maximizing the time you have to get a task done. It takes skills to be an athlete, but there are some skills with which an athlete struggles. Timing and time management were two of mine. They were not taught to me from a life or business perspective even though they often were in play on the football field, such as timing up a blitz, managing the play clock, covering wide receivers for three to five seconds, and defensive linemen and offensive linemen knowing they needed to hold or get off blocks faster or longer. In that sense, we learned about time and timing, but to see how important it was to not have any wasted space on our calendar at camp really showed how crucial time was, and it was why we got in and out of drills efficiently. They confirmed that once I was in the real world, regardless how busy I thought I was with life and business, if I structured my schedule efficiently, I would be productive.

5. Coaches made sure the expectations were **communicated** so that everyone was on the same page. This is half of the battle we face today: being able to communicate effectively. This is simply stating the message and making sure it is understood, to ensure clarity, which, finally, allows the message to be carried out. The moment we become better communicators is the moment we become fully capable of getting what we expect because now we can

cast a clear vision. Most importantly, though, the person on the other end is now able to understand what we want and how to work to make it come true. On the field, we communicated by hand signals because it was so loud you often could not hear. That kind of communication was critical for us on defense to ensure we were all in the same coverage and all moving in the right direction. If one player missed or misinterpreted the call signal, it could ruin the whole play and might even cost us the game. Understanding how important communication was on the field, then seeing it again in camp, helped me realize that this skill set is one I should strengthen. So, I constantly strive to be clear with my message for one; secondly, I make a conscious effort to effectively express myself so that my message is easily understood.

6. I **hated** doing many of the drills we went through in camp, which is probably why I learned so much from them. They made a vivid impression on me. I stayed engaged on a deeper level because I was learning more than just our football skills for the upcoming season; I also was learning life skills for the rest of my life. **To put it another way, you might not like everything you are tasked to do, but the things you don't like often are what teach you more than doing the things you like. That was my expe-**

rience. I found myself asking why we were doing that drill or this drill, but sure enough, each drill taught me something that I could use in life and business. I didn't quit just because I hated the drill. Remember this: You are never really going through, you are more like growing through.

7. If you are not **coachable**, you will fail to embrace life prep, and you will become one of those people who moan, groan, and complain and become content with whatever life or business throws at you. **Uncoachable athletes don't get to play a long time; neither do uncoachable people when it comes to business. This might be a hard pill to swallow for a lot of people, but it is the truth. If this is you, then you have a few options. 1. Get ready to be removed from the game (or the job), whether it's in sports, life, or business. 2. Get coachable and take your game to a new level. Because of my background growing up relatively poor and frequently on the move, to make it to college, I was humbled. It was because of good coaching that I had made it that far, so being coachable wasn't a problem for me. It gave me wisdom. To this day I seek out wisdom and strive to remain coachable in life and in business. Just make sure you have the right coach coaching you.**

8. In life and business, you must make **adjustments** and roll with things, just like being in the game. You know the old expression—just roll with the punches? That's what I'm talking about. If you don't do those things, the next person in line is waiting to step in and outwork you for your spot, just like on the football field. **Winners make adjustments as necessary, and losers make excuses. I learned, sometimes the hard way, that once the game is underway and things aren't going as we had game-planned, that I and others would have to make on-the-fly adjustments and not wait until halftime, because by then it might be too late. That lesson alone showed me how I was supposed to handle life and business. Regardless of the situation, there could be no excuses; just figure out the adjustments and make them. This is all that needed to be done to put me where I wanted to be in life or in business. And if I wasn't sure what those adjustments needed to be, then, I asked my teammates. In life, it could be a spouse, kids, extended family. In business, it could be business partners, managers, or staff. If you don't have the answers, ask someone for help.**

Chapter 6 Notes

SPORTS   LIFE   BUSINESS

7

STAGE FRIGHT

E VERYBODY HAS A STAGE. THAT'S WHAT THE GAME OF FOOT-
BALL SHOWED ME; it just took me awhile to realize it. In
playing the game of football for eleven years, I had become
accustomed to performing in front of people, whether it was
a hundred people in recreational ball when I was younger or
107,000 fans in Neyland Stadium during my years playing
Division I ball at Tennessee. Putting on the show and doing
what I was there to do, which was to play football (I thought),
stage fright did not bother me until I realized the purpose
of my stage was to impact, inspire, and empower those who
followed me.

Over the years of playing ball, I realized that even though
everyone has a stage, all stages aren't created equal; some are
bigger than others. The arena of sports gives you a celebrity
stage to use; whether it's local, national, or international, it's
there. The kicker is that most athletes who have these stages
develop stage fright. They fail to maximize use of their stage
during the peak of their careers, when it could assist them in

achieving their bigger purpose after they are done playing. In most cases, it's because sports is their only purpose and they don't know they have a bigger purpose (which they do). Or they just don't know how to maximize their stage, or they have been advised not to, depending on the level of the sport.

In terms of stage fright, I'm not talking about the stage of performing; you have all that handled. I'm talking about the stage fright of performing and fulfilling your **purpose** while at your peak and with all eyes on you. A great example of this is Tim Tebow, who found his purpose and exemplified it throughout his football career at the University of Florida followed by several years in the NFL. Do not wait for your career on whatever level you are on to end before deciding to do something relevant. Maximizing your stage is not the common thing to do or the popular thing to do—until you decide to do it.

As I looked around, I saw that it wasn't just people inside the game (the players), it also involved the coaches, band members, cheerleaders, the equipment managers, and water boys—all of whom had a bigger purpose for their stage. There is always someone, somewhere, who looks up to them or wants to be like them. For everyone, their stage served a purpose. Outside the game the stage is there as well, from a banker to a bus driver, from a bag boy to a building contractor, from a pencil pusher to the president of the United States; for everyone there's a stage that serves a purpose. The hardest challenge we all face, well at least for me, is realizing our stage purpose and then figuring out how to use it. Once I did that, it was learning how to leverage myself while at the peak of my stage.

Did you know you have a stage? Did you know your stage has a purpose? Are you using it?

Football was my temporary stage for my permanent purpose, and I almost lost it. I wrote earlier about how, once we moved to Arkansas, I saw football as my way *out* of Arkansas. I saw it as my chance to break the chain and a way to give my family a better life. However, I did not see it as a gift the Lord had given me so I could bring him glory. He quickly noticed and flipped my world upside down.

You are probably wondering what type of stage football gave me while I was in school. I never thought about how influential my stage was as an athlete, but I learned later it was. In high school, it gave me a platform from which I could lead my peers, from being the captain on the field to being voted Mr. CHS off the field as well. Playing football and having a stage also put me in a position of influence that allowed me to help a lot of my teammates get jobs during the offseason so they could make money when we weren't at school or in football practice. It took me a while to realize that the stage that football gave me (and other athletes) puts us in position to help boost the profiles and "coolness" quotients of other high school programs such as Future Business Leaders of America (FBLA) and student council organizations through our participation with them. As I did extra drills before and after practice, my stage showed evidence because my teammates often would be encouraged to put in extra work themselves without Coach Teddis Ingram having to ask.

So, I was using my stage, although since I didn't realize it at the time, I wasn't using it for the greater good; I didn't quite understand the purpose of my stage. I wasn't causing trouble, and I was a pretty good kid, so I figured I was using my stage correctly because God (or so I thought) was expanding it for me year after year, giving me more popularity and exposure. By the time my junior year of high school started, I felt like I had arrived. Things were happening according to my plans (but not God's plans) for my life, and that is always a problem (leaving God off to the side). I knew what I needed to do football-wise to make my dreams a reality (but not to fulfill God's purpose for my life), and these selfish thoughts would propel me to a pretty good junior year and season.

That's when God stepped in and took my stage away to remind me that it was not about me and the things I wanted; it was about what he wanted from me for his kingdom, and I had not been giving it.

That's when God stepped in and took my stage away to remind me that it was not about me and the things I wanted; it was about what he wanted from me for his kingdom, and I had not been giving it. It was a one-way street; he was doing all the giving, and I was doing all the taking and giving him no glory. Therefore, he removed my stage by allowing me to tear my ACL and miss my senior year of football. I was devastated, but now God had my attention.

Has God ever had to pull your plug to get your attention? Did it work? Of course it did. That's usually the only time we slow down to talk to God—when our world seems like it's crashing in on us. We go to him to see what he wants us to do or see what he has in store for us **after** he interrupts our stage.

My next stage was college. After having that letdown (to some degree) of using my stage in high school, I was completely aware that my notoriety, the little that I had compared to my other teammates, was not about me. At this point I believe it was about my sharing how God had taken me from the city of Atlanta, where the path I was on could have led me to becoming another statistic. Our moving to the sticks in Arkansas and my having a chance to totally focus on football, a sport that could change my family's life forever, looked very promising. Then I injured my knee and suddenly faced an uncertain future. Through it all, the Lord still made a way for me to end up at the University of Tennessee playing football, eventually on scholarship. That's the story I felt I was destined to share, and I did, to a degree, but I don't feel it was as impactful as it should have been. Maybe I was just embarrassed to share my story or the love I thought I had for the Lord. This struggle lingered on for almost two years, and then two things happened.

First, after two years of practicing and playing college football, I learned the importance of **execution**. We can practice all we want to, but if we don't **execute** the play when it's game time, nothing matters. We practiced **execution**, from our technique in the weight room to our footwork in our position skill practices, so we would not take false steps. The ability to **execute** is everything in the game of sports. Honestly, I figured it would be the same in the game of life and business as well. The law of **execution** was something I learned from the game and held on to because I knew it would be critical to me in every aspect of my life and business after my football days were done.

Second, I was introduced to the Fellowship of Christian Athletes (FCA), which helped me to grow my faith. I attended weekly . . . and not just for the free pizza from Papa John's, although, by the way, it was a great incentive. Shortly after that, my good friend and brother Inky Johnson was seriously injured. At that point, I felt my stage shifting by seeing the Lord's grace on Inky's life and how his response affected me. It was time to speak up. I had felt like I was doing a disservice to others who might have been looking up to me—especially my siblings, cousins, and younger teammates. I wasn't being a good example. I wasn't letting them know that I had been through something, only for the Lord to work it out in my favor eventually.

It was my duty to let them know that it's OK if you are going through something challenging or hurtful, because he can work it out for you if you believe in him. That was the **purpose** for my stage. The Lord was leading me into using my stage in FCA by inviting and growing my teammates to Christ. I wasn't sure how it would work, but all I could think of was to **execute**—just do it.

The time we had the largest FCA turnout for a Bible study, I felt the Lord wanted me to be the example to others there that it was cool to show and confess your love to the Lord. So that night I executed his plan for my stage and recommitted myself to my Lord and Savior, Jesus Christ, in front of the whole room. At that moment, I felt I was truly using my stage that the Lord had prepared for me to do his work. There was no longer any stage fright or embarrassment; I felt a true fulfillment of purpose on my stage.

As the next chapter of my life approached, I had to ask myself, "What do I have of value, or what skills can I bring to the table in the next phase of my life?" The first thing I thought of was football, but as I processed that thought, it turned out it really wasn't about football. I realized it was the stage that God was providing me because of football. Football was merely the temporary stage allowing me to leverage and maximize my permanent purpose to **impact**, **inspire**, and **empower** people for the glory of his kingdom.

See, I always knew God had great plans for me in life, but I assumed that it would be football related and would include the fortune that came with playing. During my last few weeks of college, God made it abundantly clear that he was working his plans for my life, and that his plans for me were to let football be my stage that got me in position to *impact, inspire, and empower* people for the glory of his kingdom. Football was a checkpoint in my life, not my destination. This is what most athletes fail to realize, which is why they miss their opportunity to capitalize on their stage when they are at the peak of their game or their stage is at its biggest. They normally do not catch this vision until coming down off the peak and their stage is no longer so big. At this point, athletes often have to seek help from people at a time when such people are no longer so eager to be associated with the athlete, who now is an ex-athlete—the cool points they once got from being associated with the athlete are no longer there.

Do what you need to do while people are interested in you because of your stage. My football career was over, but my stage wasn't. I knew I wasn't yet where God wanted me to be.

Professional football—playing in the NFL—after college didn't work out for me, but I was able to have a short-lived Professional Indoor Football League career. I knew I was at my peak in terms of football, but I knew I was destined for more as I began to transition out of the game of football. I still had my stage, though, and I knew it could be used for more while I was at my peak and before I became irrelevant.

Even though your stage isn't *about* you (or mine about me), you should use it to leverage yourself, your brand, and your name while you are at your peak. Do what you need to do while people are interested in you because of your stage. My football career was over, but my stage wasn't. I knew I wasn't yet where God wanted me to be. How did I know this? He wouldn't have been transitioning me out of football if I *was* where I needed to be; that goes for you as well. If he wanted you where you are, then he would not be moving you. Never forget that. He is just moving you while you are at your peak so you can make the biggest impact within your purpose.

It started to become clear to me that God gives everyone a stage in his or her life, regardless if they know it or if they ever intentionally use it. Our job is to find it and figure out how to use it. Our calling means not surrendering to stage fright and not going through life without truly fulfilling the purpose of your stage, a fate that happens to a lot of people. If you are alive, you have a stage; now it just depends on how big God wants to make the audience.

What I found from sports, and which I'm now noticing in life and business, is that most people fail to realize their stage and maximize it at its peak. They fail to add value to their stage, which is done by giving their crowd (the people watching them) something worthwhile to watch. They go through sports, life, or business and never let God work his plan for them because they are too busy trying to work their own plan. They are setting themselves up for disappointment and regret once they realize later in life they missed the message.

Today millions of people transition from one thing to another and believe they know what they want, and how to get it without considering their stage and its purpose. They forge ahead with no real purpose. So, what's your purpose in life after sports? It's never too early to ask yourself that question. As you start to transition in whatever area you are transitioning in, ask yourself, who is making this happen, why is it happening, and what is the purpose or bigger picture behind this happening? Is this moving me closer to or away from my purpose? These questions are to help you grasp that it is probably not you or all about you. The sooner you realize this, the faster you can embrace your stage and truly fulfill your purpose and come out of stage fright.

Some of you could be in the midst of reaching a bigger stage, or some of you could be getting your stage—your influence on behalf of God—reduced due to lack of usage. Who knows, both things could happen, first one then the other. The key is being able to conclude that you have a stage, and with that being able to say, "I brought glory to you here on earth by completing the work you gave me to do" (John 17:4). Everything you do is affecting someone in your audience, either positively or negatively. In the past, you might not have noticed it or even given it much thought, which could be the reason for your transition. It's time to allow yourself to **execute** and directly impact your crowd.

Sports, Life, Business Takeaways: Chapter 7

While reviewing the lessons presented in this chapter and summarized below, take the time to think about what early lessons, like the ones here, that you have learned in life that could benefit you in other areas. Write them down and jot down a few notes about how you can use them now, using the space to write at the end of the Takeaways.

1. Putting on the show and doing what I was there to do, which was to play football I thought, **stage fright** didn't bother me until I realized my stage was to impact, inspire, and empower those who followed me. **What I learned from football that kept me from experiencing stage fright was that I knew I was there just to do what I do, which at one point was play football. Nowadays in life and business, my purpose is to impact, inspire, and empower people to glorify the Lord's kingdom. Being clear as to the purpose of my stage allows me the opportunity to just focus on one thing, which is the execution. Now, regardless of where I'm at and what I'm doing, the purpose of my stage doesn't change, the only thing that changes is the size of the crowd watching and listening to what I do and say. Until you become clear on what your stage is, and what its true purpose is, you will experience stage**

---

fright and miss out on the true fulfillment of your purpose; it happens. That's not the end for you, though, just the beginning. Once you become comfortable with your stage and purpose for being there, you will be able to relax, deliver, and live your message more effectively. Just like you did in sports. You can do this!

2. I am talking about the stage fright of performing and fulfilling **purpose. Here is why we have one of the biggest drop-offs in terms of production once our sports careers are over or, quite frankly, when any career is over. This is because some people never find their true purpose for their stage. Once the curtains close on a stage, people feel like their lives are over or feel meaningless, as if they no longer have any relevance to society anymore; they feel useless. The truth, however, is that they are not useless; they just don't know the true purpose of their stage and might not feel fulfilled.**

3. The ability to **execute**—to get it done—is everything in sports, and I figured it would be the same in the game of life and business. **This was just a reality check for me, because as an athlete playing a sport, I know how important it is to execute the play. The importance of execution was never taught to me relative to**

other parts of my life outside of sports. I never understood how crucial of a role execution had in daily life and in business. What saved me in that regard was seeing firsthand how crucial execution was to football, and that resonated with me in a big way; I wanted to bring that same level of importance with me when it came to executing in life and business.

4. God made it ever so clear that he was working his plans for my life. His plan was to let football be my stage, which in turn got me in position to **impact, inspire**, and **empower** people for the glory of his kingdom. Football was a checkpoint in my life, not my destination. **That feeling when you finally know your stage and understand the reason for it is so rewarding—a great sense of achievement, for others within my sphere of influence as well as for me. That was one of the best things to ever happen to me and it will be for you as well. Knowing all this allowed me to execute, regardless of where God took me and put me. I knew my purpose on my stage and all I had to do was focus on executing. Still, to this day, with all the travel and business that I do, I understand that wherever I am, the purpose doesn't change, only the size of the crowd.**

Chapter 7 Notes

_____

_____

_____

_____

_____

_____

_____

_____

_____

_____

_____

_____

_____

_____

8

THE TRANSITION

O F ALL THE TRANSITIONS I'VE BEEN THROUGH—TO INCLUDE hopping from school to school during my mom's many moves around Atlanta while I was growing up—the biggest transition was when I went from college into the real world; facing life after sports. As a college athlete, I got to see athletes in all major collegiate sports put all their eggs in one basket. They were dependent on making it in professional sports because they didn't know what else they wanted to do in life or what their identity was outside of their sport.

There were even the everyday students who would change their major so they could prolong graduation and stay in school longer. That's because they, too, didn't know what they wanted to do. I even saw numerous guys leaving school early (in terms of graduating) for the NFL, only to not make it at all or to not have these long luxurious careers that we all dream about. They find themselves returning to school to finish their degree. This might sound great in that latter case, but their motive for coming back wasn't quite what you might have expected. They weren't coming back to finish because they wanted it or needed it for a particular degree and career. Most were returning to school to buy time because they were not sure what was next or how to **transition** into the real world of life after sports. That's sad, but it's the reality if you don't know what's next.

That's when it begins to sink in: **"There comes a moment where all good things end so that great things can begin. (IIE)."** That moment is the transition that is the focal point of this book, whether it's a transition from high school to college, college to the work force, pro athlete to the real world work force to becoming an entrepreneur, single status to marriage and family, or vice versa on that last one. Each time we make a transition, it's as if we are entering a new world and we have to learn, adapt, and change our ways of doing things from what we have become familiar with for months, years, or decades. During these transitions, some people don't skip a beat and transition smoothly. On the other hand, from what I noticed, most people struggle with transitioning on almost every level—some more than others. Plus, the degree of struggle can vary on different levels, depending on the magnitude of how the transition is perceived. All I know is that the "transition trap," as common as it is, was not going to get me. My hope is that after you have finished reading this book, you will have learned a principle or two (or three or more) that will help you avoid the transition trap and make your next transition in sports, life, or business your best one ever.

The process of changing from one position to another defines **transition**. This period of our lives is often pivotal

There comes a moment where all good things end so that great things can begin.

to our success, but yet it is one of the least-taught fundamentals of life. I had a crash course on transitioning as I grew up, with all the moving around we did. Through repetition and what sports taught me, I acquired some insight into making a smooth transition. Depending on your sport, the principle of **transition** is something everyone learns and learns early. Think about it. When **transitioning** from one football practice drill to another, you are taught to hustle, run, sprint, jog . . . whatever you need to do to do it quickly. There was never a time I was told to take my sweet time going to the next drill. This is something we often do because we are either tired, unexcited, or just do not want to go on to the next drill because it scares us. That's a lot like transitioning in life or business.

When the transition is something we are excited about, we move faster; but if it's something we do not want to move on from, we take our time. This hinders us in the long run. Learning that lesson in football, I took heed. Psychologically, hustling from station to station on the field made me feel prepared, and it forced me to get my mind right faster. Whatever it was, it worked. Since it worked on the football field for me, I figured it would help produce some results for me when real life and business kicked in.

I knew I had to transition my mind before I transitioned my grind.

Let me discuss a few more of those lessons that helped me transition like a champion. First was the **Identity** transition, **"I knew I had to transition my mind before I transitioned my grind"** (IIE). Playing sports most of my life instilled in me that whatever my new role would be, I had to embody it, embrace it, look the part, and act the part. No more "D.low, the athlete," even though that's how people wanted to perceive me and still do to this day, depending on when and where we first got to know each other.

Early on in my young-adult life, I believed my career path would be one with entrepreneurship as my destination. That would give me the freedom to maximize my earning potential and create the life I wanted to live. I had to go to work to be known as "D.low the businessman" if I was going to be my own boss. I began experimenting with building my businessman brand my junior year in college. I had no idea what I was doing, so I started with how I dressed myself, albeit with some limitations.

I owned only two suits at the time, so instead of making excuses for not having clothes, I took out a student loan and revamped my wardrobe. No more the casual look of an athlete for me. I dressed up in a suit and tie every day for class that year just to see if I could do it and to also

How you are perceived is how you are received.

see how I would be perceived. What I learned was, **"How you are perceived is how you are received (IIE)."** It was interesting to see the reactions of people when they found out I played football but wasn't dressed like a college jock. Professors who didn't know I played sports even treated me differently; they didn't stereotype me as an athlete when it came to class participation, homework, or class assignments. Of course, the only question fellow student-athletes asked me much of the time was, "Why are you so dressed up?" I would simply reply, "I have a business meeting later."

I was **transitioning** my mind to the business-meeting grind. Still to this day, that's how my peers and many others from that period of my life remember me: the guy who wore suits to class. I realized early that **"Everything you do is an interview for the next thing you're going to do (IIE)."**

Looking the part came easy for me after I had enough clothes to wear, but acting the part still required some effort. Some of the things that came to mind: How do business-men act? What do they do? I needed to find a way (or an excuse) to get around them and rub elbows with them more. I wanted to be around them so much that they would see me as their peer, like the athletes were to me. I needed to identify with them so they could identify with me and welcome me into their environment. So that's what I did every night. Instead of watching TV, I found (tasteful) bars, restaurants, and net-working events to attend that would put me around busi-nessmen. I learned to walk their walk and talk their talk until they saw me as "D.low, the businessman," not "D.low the athlete."

Everything you do is an interview for the next thing you're going to do.

The first thing you must do during your **transition** is re-lease yourself from **"identity jail."** Stop hold-ing yourself hostage to the only identity you know of yourself and explore your new reality. **"Your mind is the only thing holding you back (IIE)."**

Your mind is the only thing holding you back.

In identity jail, you set your own bond. When you hold yourself hostage, you set your own ransom. Understanding this is when I became free. Now that I was free in my mind, I could be free with my grind. The grind I refer to is to be more, do more, have more than what society had planned for me and what everyone thought athletes were sup-posed to be. No one broke the mold for me; I did it myself. By applying what I knew from the game, the transition was not as difficult for me as I had seen with my peers. Why? I be-lieve mainly it was because of some earlier life philosophies

119

that I had learned and embodied, which years later molded me into the person I needed to become during that moment in my life.

When it came down to the transitions I made in my life, I was mentally prepared. Each transition took me to the next level in being prepared for one to follow. I stacked one experience on top of another. I felt that put me ahead of the game, and you can do the same for yourself. It starts with embracing transition, not fearing it. That's what football taught me, how to mentally **prepare**. Not **prepare** in the sense of what's next but more in the form of my ability to have multiple titles, jobs, obligations, and responsibilities. What I mean by this is I can always remember playing multiple positions while growing up, playing multiple sports. In football, it was running back and safety. I did completely different tasks on opposite sides of the ball. In basketball, it was small forward or power forward, but also made sure I was the best defender on the other end of the court

As I got to college, the pecking order of priorities was being student first, athlete second. Those were two completely different types of roles I was required to perform. Putting the student part before the athlete part helped me mentally prepare and confirmed to me that I was more than just an athlete. I was capable of more than just football. It validated to me that I could do more, be more, and contribute more to this world than just athletic ability. Knowing I was capable of more than just one thing is what gave my mind the winning edge when the transitions from life and business began to manifest themselves for me. I was prepared. Are you prepared? If not, start now. I've already told you some about how I did it, like using a student loan to expand my business wardrobe. What's your next move?

Here are more of those principles I applied to my life to "transition like a champ" from the *The Transition PlayBook* curriculum I created that will help everyone you know avoid the transition trap. (The curriculum is available in a separate publication and is meant to be purchased as a companion to this book.)

- Next was the law of the **"Carryover,"** which also can be referred to as the "same as" principle. **The idea behind this principle is that once you're successful on the field, you can take that success and those principles or psychology that made you successful and carry them over into another field or endeavor.** Did extra prep make you more successful on the field or in the gym? If so, it makes sense to apply that to your post-sports career. Or, maybe it was developing a great rapport with teammates and coaches, and in the process learning how to share and soak up wisdom from others. Make that work in your professional life, too. When doing so, you will stand to produce the same outcome of success in business. I knew of too many athletes who lost their fight, skill set, and will to win during their transition from college to the workforce, or from the pros to the "after life" as average Joes. This was all for the lack of knowing how to **carry over** the skills they had worked their lives to develop. They came to believe those skills were no longer of value and would have to be completely abandoned when transitioning into their new career. That's wrong thinking. **In my case, I had to ask myself a few questions: What principles did I learn, and how do I take them and apply them to this new**

life? These were tough but rewarding questions as I figured out the answers. What these answers did was solidify the next step for me. The basis for this is **"Know what you know."** That means whatever it is that you did or that you are doing, you should by now have mastered that skill set or some skills from that craft. Then at any given time, and without any doubt, you should have confidence in yourself to perform that skill or skill sets that you either learned or were naturally bestowed with. With me it was networking—having the ability to meet and connect with people. I knew that skill without a smidgen of doubt, so when it was time for me to make a transition from sports into the business world, I knew where my confidence resided and that it was a matter of entering a career field where my confidence would readily apply.

- **Starting with my strength** of networking, and what I knew, made it easier for me when I got into sales. Starting off your transition with your strength will also make it easier for you as well. I gravitate toward positions that involve people, since I understand things about people and establishing relationships. This allowed me to carry over my networking skills. It also made it clear to me the things I needed to **learn** in sales, because my past hadn't offered any experience in those areas. Knowing what I know was a game changer for me and made me aware of the learning curve ahead or lack thereof as I transitioned. **Knowing what you know** will be a game changer for you as well; now you will have inventory of your strengths and can work to sharpen them while being aware of your weaknesses (we all have them, trust me). This will allow you to sharpen skills while giving yourself a chance to learn or study others who are stronger in your weaker areas. It's knowing what you know. In football, I knew there were always ten other guys on the field with me. We all had strengths and weaknesses, but together we were solid. In that team process, I had a chance to develop and be stronger all the way around by studying and practicing with my teammates.

- The last thing I did was **"seek wisdom,"** which is knowledge of what is true. In reading the Bible, I came across Scripture talking about the wise men. Every few chapters in the Bible it said to "seek wisdom," and I would see the word 'wisdom' so much that it began to stand out for me. I figured I would listen more to others and sift through what I heard, seeking pearls of wisdom. I advise you to do the same, to include reading Scripture. Pay attention to what you read and hold on to what you hear! Make notes if you must. You might be wondering, "How do I seek wisdom?" Simple: get advice from those with expertise in your field. Read books—learn from those who have been where you are planning to go. Learn from those who are living the way you want to live morally, spiritually, and financially. Learn from the people carrying themselves in the manner you want to carry yourself. Learn from the people who have the types of relationships with their spouse, kids, family, employer, employees, and business partners that you want to have. This is how you seek wisdom. It worked for me, and I am confident it will work for you as you avoid the transition trap. You know what I'm talking about, right? Remember what I earlier wrote about buying business suits and going to bars, restaurants, and networking events to meet other business people and learn from them while letting them get to know you? I was seeking wisdom.

I just knew there had to be something out there—a book or some other type of resource—that would serve as a blueprint to transitioning from sports into life and business. I was wrong. In my search, I found plenty of scattered quotes and accounts in which people shared about what sports had taught them and how they might have used a tidbit of advice here and there from sports to apply to business. However, there was nothing out there—or at least that I'm aware of—that correlates sports and all its lessons in a consolidated, practical guide to living life and conducting business or a career beyond sports. I found nothing that would make the sports-to-life-business transition a heck of a lot easier. That's why I created the *(SLB) Sports Life Business: The Transition PlayBook* curriculum, which is the new standard for transitioning like a champion. Earlier here you had a chance to learn some of the basic principles that anyone, anywhere can pick up and transition whenever and wherever they are in sports, in life, or in business.

The *(SLB) Sports Life Business: The Transition PlayBook* curriculum is composed of the skills, philosophies, and psychology of those athletes who dominated in their arena, then transitioned into life and business with just as much domination. That's what you are going to receive if you pick up the SLB curriculum; the new standard for transitioning. It will show you "how to transition like a champion" as you make your journey through sports, life, and business.

These types of philosophies are what I wish they would teach in school. You will find this accumulated knowledge here as you continue your journey through sports, life, and business, because they all come together. I hope you paid close attention as I shared with you how I avoided the transition trap during my journey. Hopefully, you can apply the same principles I applied and continue to use in my own life, and you will get mega results. For those who are currently struggling with transitioning in any area of sports, life, or business, go to www.sportslifebusiness.com for a detailed blueprint and purchase a copy of *(SLB) Sports Life Business: The Transition PlayBook.*

Sports, Life, Business Takeaways: Chapter 8

While reviewing the lessons presented in this chapter and summarized below, take the time to think about what early lessons, like the ones here, that you have learned in life that could benefit you in other areas. Write them down and jot down a few notes about how you can use them now, using the space to write at the end of the Takeaways.

1. Professional athletes leaving their respective sports often return to school to bide their time because they're not sure what's next or how to **transition** into the real world or life after sports. **After seeing this happen to so many athletes at other schools and to some with whom I played, I knew this was not an option for me, but I wasn't sure about my current team or classmates, so I knew I had to find an answer. Well, there is no better way to find an answer than to become the answer. Since I knew from the time I was in college that it would be a problem down the road, I began to prepare as if it would be my problem. That's when the answers began to flow and concepts for all the things I'd learned from moving and football came to me.**

2. The first transition was the identity transition, **"I knew I had to transition my mind before I transitioned my grind (IIE)." This is probably**

the hardest but most overlooked step for athletes—seeing yourself for what you have been and not for what you are becoming. It's not a matter of looking at yourself as a has-been; it's more like, "I've been there and done that," and this is the basis for what is next for you to achieve. The quicker you make this transition, the faster you can begin to find your new/true identity.

3. **You should carry over** your skills that you have worked your entire life to develop. Don't abandon them when transitioning into your new career—they will continue to serve you well as there must be at least one or two skills that you can readily adapt. **With carryover, you do not have to abandon your skills as long as you make a transition into an area in which you can apply them. Then ask yourself a few questions: "What principles and skills did I learn, and how do I take them and apply them to this?"** Based on those answers, you will know what you can carry over and what you should not. It's not complicated.

4. **Know what you know.** Whatever it is that you did, or that you are currently doing, you should have mastered a skill set or some skills from that craft. We all have mastered at least one skill or another. If you don't think so, you haven't looked hard enough. At any given time, without any

doubt, you have good reason to have confidence in yourself to perform that skill or skill set that you either learned or were naturally bestowed with. **Start with your strength(s). This alone will give you confidence out the gate and confidence in yourself to boost what you believe and produce for you what will be an advantage in your new environment. A coach once told me, "I'd rather have you going full speed in the wrong direction than have you going slow in the right one." Hopefully, that won't be your case, but if so, all you must do is turn yourself around. From there, you will be on your way to success.**

5. **Seek wisdom,** which is knowledge of what is true. **This to me is one of the best learning routes to success in anything you do. This gives you the ability to learn from others' successes and mistakes. Never take wisdom for granted, and seek it relentlessly.** Here is some wisdom I acquired along my transition: **Do not do this alone; do not think you know it all; do not be afraid to ask for help; do not be afraid to ask questions of qualified professionals; do not get overwhelmed; do not rush the process; do not lie to yourself; do not move backward; do not doubt yourself; do not cheat yourself; do not quit.**

6. Football taught me how to **prepare** mentally.

Not **prepare** in the form of what's next but more in the form of my ability to have multiple titles, jobs, obligations, and responsibilities. It's called multitasking. **I never really thought about this lesson until the time came in my first sales role, where I had to do multiple tasks within the course of the sale. I had to meet prospects, greet them, warm up with them, ask discovering questions—all the while making them like me while I presented a product that I was going to ask them to buy, when in most cases they did not yet realize they needed my product. The ability to prepare gave me confidence that I had held multiple responsibilities before and had success, so I could do it again.**

7. Release yourself from the **"identity jail."** Stop holding yourself hostage to the only identity you know of and explore your new reality. **"Your mind is the only thing holding you back. (IIE)."**

Chapter 8 Notes

_____

_____

_____

_____

_____

_____

_____

_____

_____

_____

_____

_____

_____

_____

SPORTS   LIFE   BUSINESS

9

SACRIFICE

S ACRIFICE IS TO SURRENDER OR GIVE FOR THE SAKE OF SOME-
THING ELSE. **"All roads lead to a sacrifice in sports, in
life, and in business if you want success (IIE)."**

I learned from sports that sacrifice comes in the form of
many things. Some sacrifices come in actions, places, emotions, ways, or things, but the strongest sacrifice of them all
is the ability to sacrifice beliefs. Throughout my football-
playing days, I learned to sacrifice on many different levels.
The one that has served me the most, and the one which I
believe most athletes and people miss, is the **ability to sacrifice disempowering beliefs**. The lesson of sacrifice is embodied all throughout sports, but it's never actually
acknowledged that it is being taught, so once you have finished playing, one of the most valuable lessons you can take
with you into life and business is left behind because you
never knew you learned it. **"Sports can teach you a lot, but
it does not matter if you miss the message"** (IIE).

Among the most valuable lessons I learned from the game relative to the sacrifice of disempowering beliefs that can be applied in life and business was my **ability to sacrifice fear—to put it out of my thoughts**. I remember my early football days and the fear that came from making contact while going full speed. It was the fear of getting hurt; I would always slow down right before contact to protect myself. That is, until one game, when I was blocking (not one of my strong points), and I completely got my head knocked off, and the play was ruined. I wasn't hurt physically, but my pride was damaged.

Instead of taking me out of the game, Coach called the exact same play. At this point, I knew that either the same thing was going to happen or I was going to get it together. I figured I would just go full speed ahead and run through whoever came to block me. Once the ball was snapped, I ran through the hole—mad, angry, and nervous, all at the same time—looking for someone to hit. Guess what; this time they all moved out of my way, which created a wide-open hole through which my fullback could score.

At that moment, I learned something. I learned that fear is fake; it had made me relent from going full speed in the game . . . until I decided to sacrifice my fear and its fabricated outcome. This ability to sacrifice—to get rid of—fear in life and in business is vital, to be used in whatever situations with irrational outcomes that we can formulate in our minds.

The next critical lesson was **sacrificing my ability to quit**. In football, you never give up; you play until the clock strikes 0:00. This alone is internalized, so whatever I start, I do until completion or until the clock runs out. Not completing the task to the prearranged finishing point goes against everything in me. This lesson adds value to my business dealings because it makes me evaluate tasks thoroughly before taking them on.

The next lesson was **sacrificing the ability to doubt myself**. Playing and competing in the Southeastern Conference was a matter of survival—day to day, week to week, season to season. It was intense in ways that someone who never played college football could never fathom. By playing SEC football, I could no longer doubt what I was capable of achieving.

Then I learned the **ability to sacrifice complaining**. No griping; just suck it up and do it. This one was hard to learn and abide by—to this day it still takes focus, but I truly had to look at the opportunities that were granted to me to realize that despite how things are or might seem, there's always someone who would die to trade places with me. This puts it all in perspective.

Another lesson is one I learned as a kid and which helped me get to the University of Tennessee, and it is one I will always carry with me: the ability to **sacrifice cheating the process and myself**. Sacrifice means giving it up—letting it go. There are no shortcuts to the top. Just put in the work and let the work, work itself out.

Finally, there's the ability to **sacrifice blame** and be responsible for my own life. I once heard a coach say, "If it is to be, it's up to me." Once I heard that, I knew I could no longer blame someone else for my success or lack thereof.

I caught on quick that sacrifices would come either by choice or by force. Either you will start doing what it takes to make it, or you won't make it because you will keep doing what you were doing. That was the example I saw repeatedly from guys growing up who had more talent than me in every sport I played, but they never developed and took their talents past high school because they weren't **willing to sacrifice the now for later**. That chance you take, that decision you make, that attitude you have today, will affect the rest of your life, so be willing to live with it.

Growing up, I didn't think about it as much because, like almost everyone else, I sacrificed by being forced to. Once I got to college, though, I started to sacrifice by choice. Honestly, I figured after all that I had sacrificed in college—my time, my energy, my effort, my focus, my discipline, my body, my freedom, my actions—it could only get easier from there. Those were all things I sacrificed for the privilege of playing football at the University of Tennessee. I believed that anything I did afterward in life would be easier compared to the sacrifices I made playing D1 level football in the SEC. That's why I felt confident that success in everything after football was inevitable.

At least, that's what I conditioned myself to believe. Here's why: For four years at UT, I had my life scheduled for me. You can see it from the photos of my fall camp schedule and daily schedule in chapter 6. The first half of my day was centered around classes and working toward grades that would either stay the same, improve, or worsen over the course of my collegiate career; fortunately, mine improved.

The day I saw what my schedule looked like, I knew something had to go. There was too much work to be done in the classroom and on the field, and no time for frivolous distractions, even though they didn't feel too frivolous at the time—just the normal fun stuff a teen likes to do. Remember, though, I still did not have a scholarship. I would have to bust my tail to earn one to be able to get to where I wanted to go. I knew I was going to have to give up something. " **I had to be willing to invest short-term pain for long-term gain. I** had made it to Tennessee, so now it was up to me to finish the task.

Let me make it clear: sacrifice doesn't just mean to *stop* doing things; often, it means having to *start* doing things. In my case I needed to start doing a lot of things that weren't optional; it was just a matter of what I needed to do, and when I needed to do it. I knew **sacrifice** was required for my advancement. Purpose and hope followed up by massive action would be needed for me to advance. It would require more sacrifice on my part than it would for most of my teammates who already had their keep (a football scholarship). I suppose I could have been observing what they were or were not doing, compare it to where I was, and from that determine what I needed to do. Often, however, that's what hinders people from staying committed to sacrifices—they are too busy trying to fit in and do what everyone else is doing, when they should be focused solely on what they know they must do, on their own. **"To fit in with the successful, you've got to stand out like the successful (IIE)."** This needs to be exemplified daily.

> *To fit in with the successful, you've got to stand out like the successful.*

Sacrifice is not a popularity contest; it's more like the ugly duckling no one wants or wants anything to do with—until they see the outcome and it's a beautiful swan. Sacrificing my time was the first thing I had to handle. My schedule would be filled with classes and practice, so the first thing I sacrificed was signing up for "easy" courses to fill my electives requirements—you know, fun classes you take to boost your GPA without having to do much work, yet they really aren't worth anything nor do they help you graduate. First order of business: make sure those easy electives weren't on my schedule. I wanted to put all my energy into classes that counted for my major and which worked around my football schedule. To this day, this is how I prioritize my life and business: do the stuff that matters, and stop worrying about stuff that doesn't. Put the time and energy into the important things first.

I knew football practice and proving myself would take effort, but so would classes. I wasn't a genius, so I had to apply extra effort to keep my grades right, because they had gotten me in the door at Tennessee. That meant I needed to maximize the resources that were provided, and that took focus. There were plenty of things in college that I wanted to let distract me early on, but I kept remembering, "Sacrifice now for later." When I wasn't working on improving my football skills, my focus shifted back to the two Gs, grades and girls. That wasn't bad, because I made sure they were smart girls who could help me with my grades. I had no time to experiment with drinking or drugs because they would not bring me closer to the outcome I wanted. I helped myself by starting to set goals. I asked myself, **"What do I want?"** Then, **"What actions can I take to help move me toward that desired outcome? What actions will move me away?"** Those simple questions were my road map, showing me what sacrifices I had to make—what I should be doing versus what I shouldn't be doing. Even now, this formula predicated on those questions still guides me in everything I do. The hardest part is not asking the questions; it is following through once you get the answers.

The next thing I learned to **sacrifice** came after our football workouts. Not only did the workouts **discipline** our bodies, they taught me how to **discipline** my mind. I had to change my diet, because it made no sense to put my body through the ringer with our workouts but not get maximum results because of my taste for crap (not literally, but you know what I mean—junk food). If I was going to **sacrifice** through the pain of those required workouts to take care of my outsides in the physical sense, I figured I should take just as good care of my insides as well.

I was willing to **sacrifice** whatever it took to make it happen. The commitment it was going to take for me to make it on the field while getting my full scholarship was going to require me to sacrifice my personal freedom; I needed to be consumed with the process. Being young and having personal freedom most of my life, especially growing up, I had never had to truly commit to anything of this magnitude. I didn't like that idea, but I understood if I sacrificed and took the right actions, that all this hard work would pay off and my pain would not be in vain. The risk was worth the reward; I just needed to make the play.

The reason everyone is not as successful as they can be is because they are not willing to make the tough sacrifices for the period of time necessary to achieve the desired outcome.

Football continued to give me early, helped me to realize that the road to your dreams goes through sacrifice. I learned that if sacrifice were not a prerequisite for success, everyone would be successful to a higher degree. The reason everyone is not as successful as they can be is because **they are not willing to make the tough sacrifices for the period of time necessary to achieve the desired outcome.**

Sacrifice is that test you take along your journey that whispers to you, "Is this really what I want, or would I be more comfortable staying where I am?" Most people only sacrifice **when the pain of staying the same outweighs the pain of change.** That's when we typically commit to making sacrifices however we need to. When we think of sacrifices, we usually begin by thinking of the big things we need to change, like radically changing our diet to get healthier, but what I learned from football is that it is often the really small sacrifices, the tiny adjustments, that are a lot easier to make and which often make the biggest difference. We have the tendency to look at the big picture versus that one small detail that could alter the big picture.

One of my favorites coaches, Monte Kiffin, once told me, **"You see a little, you see a lot; you see a lot, you see nothing,"** and that lesson has stuck with me and helped me fight the sacrifice struggle. If you see the small sacrifice, you can get to where you want to go. It might seem insignificant, but it also appears more attainable. However, the moment you realize there are some big changes, the tendency is to be overwhelmed and take on more than you are prepared to handle. Those sacrifices tend to be short-lived—difficult to stick with. Once you start seeing differences being made based on small sacrifices, it reassures your decision. In turn, it will eventually make the big things seem small and therefore more attainable to sacrifice. Learning the law of sacrifice has propelled me in life and business in situations that would have been difficult to deal with if I hadn't already learned and been applying this lesson, carrying it with me from the game of football into my life.

Sports, Life, Business Takeaways: Chapter 9

While reviewing the lessons presented in this chapter and summarized below, take the time to think about what early lessons, like the ones here, that you have learned in life that could benefit you in other areas. Write them down and jot down a few notes about how you can use them now, using the space to write at the end of the Takeaways.

1. **Sacrifice** is to surrender or give for the sake of something greater. I learned from sports that **sacrifice** comes in the form of many things; some come in actions, places, emotions, ways, or things. **Knowing that all sacrifice does not look the same made it easier to notice areas in which I needed to sacrifice. Failure to understand just that one thing can give someone who desires change or improvements a sense of false hope if they can't also call out their areas of sacrifice. Those areas where sacrifice is called for pop up on a consistent basis on my journey through life and in business. However, this knowledge of knowing that sacrifices can and will look different does not mean they are. A sacrifice is a sacrifice, regardless how it looks.**

2. I believe most athletes and people miss out on the **ability to sacrifice disempowering beliefs. It's not intentional. It's just easy to miss out**

because it's not something specifically brought to your attention. You are learning indirectly through drills and fundamental lessons or skills you need for the game. When their playing days are over, most athletes only remember the drill they performed, not the by-product—the lesson—learned from the drill.

3. **"Sports can teach you a lot, but it doesn't matter if you miss the message (IIE)."** That's why I was afforded the opportunity to write this book, because there is such a high percentage of athletes and other people who miss their lessons from the game of sports, the game of life, or the game of business. I just want the person who reads this book, once they put it down, to able to say it got them one step closer to their dreams in sports, in life, or in business by making them aware of the message spoken through the lessons they are exposed to every day.

4. **Sacrificing the ability to doubt myself was essential for survival while playing football in the SEC.** After four years of playing SEC football, I could no longer doubt what I was capable of achieving. That's how confident I was in myself after having survived the SEC "wars." **There are just some things that you needn't waste your time on—doubting yourself and your ability is one of them. I'm grateful for the level of competition that takes place in college**

football, especially in the SEC. This level of competition raised the bar for my performance; in fact, it not only raised the bar for me and what I expected of myself but also for what other people expected of me. That was a blessing. That level of achievement is not one that just anyone can reach. After going through something like that, you feel that you should always be able to rise above and beyond standard achievement en route to reaching elite level. The confidence of knowing that is what has helped me sacrifice my doubt, and to this day that is a renewing sacrifice.

5. I learned the ability to sacrifice complaining— to give it up. One of my favorite quotes starts out with the phrase "As long as you have breath, never complain or pout. . . ." The first time I saw that, I realized everything I was facing at that time in sports and my life was a blessing; it could always be a lot worse; for one thing, I could be dead. That sacrifice helped me become more thankful for every opportunity I had to play football. Now it makes me grateful for the opportunity to live life and grow my business, no matter how bad things might seem.

6. Another thing I will always carry with me is the ability to **sacrifice cheating the process and myself.** You just can't do it; nothing good can

happen to you or for you if you cheat or skip the process in sports, in life, or in business. The process will always catch up to you, meaning the truth will come out eventually.

7. There's also the ability to **sacrifice blame** and be responsible for my own life. Don't blame others; be accountable. **It is so easy to blame your lack of playing time, lack of recruitment, or lack of winning in sports on someone or something else, but at some point, the game will end, and life and busy-ness will begin, and you will have a fresh start to make it happen. This is where most people won't capitalize because they will miss the opportunity. They will be too busy blaming someone for their lack of opportunity. I am thankful I learned that blaming others never got anything accomplished. I could start taking responsibility for my own life and business. My success or failure wasn't in anyone else's hands but my own.**

Chapter 9 Notes

_____

_____

_____

_____

_____

_____

_____

_____

_____

_____

_____

_____

_____

_____

_____

_____

SPORTS   LIFE   BUSINESS

10

BIGGER THAN YOU

WHEN I LOOK BACK AT IT ALL, THE WRITING ON THE WALL shows me that my life and everything I had endured was for a cause much bigger than me. Jesus showed us the way when he died on a cross for something bigger than him. To him, the salvation of mankind was worth his life. The message has always been there; we just often miss it.

The sports stage alone was the stage with which the Lord blessed me so that I could do his work, which was for something bigger than me—his kingdom—and for that I was grateful. It took me awhile to realize that and I'm grateful I realized it before he took my football stage away permanently. You see it every day if you look around; someone loaded with all kinds of talent and they have wasted it. Or maybe they didn't waste it; maybe they just never realized that their stage was bigger than them, and the Lord took it away before they had a chance to negatively impact the crowd that was meant to be influenced by them. Don't get me wrong: the crowd still learned something from this person's performance, but the lesson was more like, this is what happens if you don't realize it's bigger than you.

This is one of the most missed-out-on lessons that sports teaches, and the only way to prevent becoming a victim of not realizing it's bigger than you (like I almost did), is to ask yourself, **"Who (or what) am I playing for?"** This is the question whether it involves sports, life, or business. So, what's the answer? My wife? My mom? My dad? Myself? My situation? My kids? My grandparents? My livelihood? God? My employer? An investor? My business partner? Who? Regardless of what your answer(s) is/are, I'm guessing you said that you were playing/conducting your sport/life/business for more than yourself, just confirming you are playing for a cause or a reason bigger then you.

When I think about the game of football and all that I gave it and all that I took from it, I begin to see how the game was so much bigger than me. In the big picture, I was only a piece of it, doing my part to make sure the game lived on and to give it my two cents that would hopefully make it better for the guys who came after me. The guys that played the game before me did their part, laying down the foundation and setting the tone for how the game was supposed to be played in the SEC and at the University of Tennessee. My job was to follow their lead on how to play the game as well as to raise the bar for what is expected and what is possible. For a student-athlete going under a microscope, that threshold is getting finer and finer (i.e., tougher and tougher, lesser room for error).

I believe the players in my era were there to redefine the lines. Now we see younger guys coming in behind me to go on and do things you would not think were possible in a classroom academically and on a football field athletically.

This is humbling. I feel grateful to have played a small part in such a big picture for those guys because the story and the legacy live on through them. Once you understand it's bigger than you are, you can truly focus in on what it's all about—**honor and legacy**, as Inky would say. **It's all about honoring those who came before you and paving a way to leave a legacy for those who come behind you.** That's one of the first things the game taught me; the more I learned, the more I realized that was a formula for life as well—carrying on a legacy and then passing it along in better shape than you got it. Now as the game is over for me, and I charge through life, everything I do I have a true understanding that it is bigger than me. Following are a few clues the Lord showed me in making it clear to me over and over in everything I did, in sports, in life, and in business, that whatever circumstance I'm in, it is bigger than me.

It's all about honoring those who came before you and paving a way to leave a legacy for those who come behind you. That's one of the first things the game taught me.

There's the concept of **team**, where you have individuals who are competing for their own self-worth at the same time they are answering the call to come together with others to compete as one unit while moving toward a common goal. Once winning and losing started to **really** matter, every coach I ever had, adopted this concept of **doing what is best for the TEAM.** That's always the overarching theme of a coach's message, whether they communicate it thoroughly or not. The coach's actions will always show it; that's why certain kids start and some ride the bench. That's why you have star players and role players. When the game is on the line, it's the star players the coach is calling on because they are the best people to depend on to ensure the **team** wins. It's bigger than you (unless you are the star in this case). Even if you compete individually but are on a team such as track, you can score all the points but the win goes to the *team*, which is just another clue that it is bigger than you.

The **team** concept was not new to me when I got to college, but in the daily grind of climbing my own personal mountains, I would find myself caught up in wanting to do what was best for *me*. We all have been there; in some cases, it could even seem like the coach does not have your best interests in mind; "they don't like me," or whatever we tell ourselves. Regardless of whether a coach liked me or not, I had to realize that it wasn't about me. During our personal struggles, doubts, setbacks, setups, comebacks, letdowns, breakups, successes, or failures in your sport, in your life, or in your business—whatever—we tend to forget that there's one thing we should always remember—it's bigger than me.

This is by far the biggest lesson that football taught me; proving to me that my journey was bigger than me. Football provided me the option of having an expressway to my dreams, but God took me off the expressway and put me on the scenic route. Back then I didn't get it, but now I understand it; it was all bigger than me. He was setting me on the road to learn, to endure, and to see what I needed to see and what I needed to know so that days, weeks, months, years later down the road, I would be able to relate to the people who came after me.

Those people who started on the highway to their dreams but ended up on a byway (I got here "by way" of this or "by way" of that) likely had planned to make their dreams come true, like I did, regardless of the route they had to take. This is why the Lord did not let me quit along the way or take a different exit; I had to stay on the scenic route because it was bigger than me. On my route, I saw a lot of exits that I could have taken (Who knows where I would have ended up?). Thank goodness, I stay the course each time until I reach my destination. Just know that with each exit that caught my attention, there was a roadblock or something else that detoured me from taking that (wrong) exit. I stayed the course, not thinking about it at the time, but if I had changed my course, it would have changed the message for those coming behind me. Because once I got to my destination, which was the University of Tennessee, the available detours still didn't stop. There were times when I asked myself if earning my scholarship had been worth all this: "Maybe I should transfer—I know plenty of schools that would take me right now on scholarship." But with the grace of the Lord, I stuck it out because he knew it was bigger than me.

My enduring the process would eliminate the excuses of my nieces, nephews, younger cousins, younger brother, younger sister, future children, and anyone who admires me and is coming behind me will not be able to say that Derrick Furlow Jr. had taken the easy route. When things get hard, because they will, they will not be able to say, "But you went to Tennessee." I will be able to look them in the eye and say, "I took the scenic route. No, it wasn't easy, but I made it. And if I can make it, you can make it, so do not tell me it can't be done." My route might not have been the same route as the one they are now taking, and their process might not be relatable to what I experienced during the process, but what I can do in the here and now is share with them that it was a process, and the process is bigger than them.

You must go through something to get to something. Having gone through the part where I had to learn how the game was bigger than me, I can reflect back to see how *life* was bigger than me as well. That said, walk with me as I take you down the road of clues that life throws at you.

When you are a kid, it's funny how your parents name you and it's all about you. They even make you feel special with your first name. They call you "Little Derrick," so everything you do is "Little Derrick this," "Little Derrick that." As you get older, the "Little" goes away. Now it's just "Derrick," and the things you are doing aren't as cute as they were when you were little. Over a period of time, you become a teenager, and you want this and you want that, and then you hear these words, "Everything is not all about you, Derrick." That's normally the first clue, that everything isn't about you, but you miss it.

You continue to grow up and then go to college, and on the first day of college classes your professor addresses you by your last name while checking attendance and refers to you by your last name for the rest of the semester. That's the **second clue your first name is not as important as your last name.** Your last name is bigger than you because it will outlive you. At football practice, the coaches and even your teammates (via peer pressure) are pushing you to exhaustion during workouts to see if you are going to quit on them when the game is on the line in the fourth quarter and its fourth down with three seconds left, and you are just short of the goal line in the championship game, and they are depending on someone to set up and make a play. That's the third clue. Finally, "Derrick" is graduated, now entering the workforce, soon to be married and be a future father, and the light bulb comes on. It's not about Derrick; it is much bigger than Derrick.

At this point you are probably saying to yourself, "It *is* my life. Of course it's about me," You're 100 percent right. **It is about you in a sense, but everything that you do will**

directly or indirectly affect someone around you at some point. Choices, decisions, actions (or lack thereof), attitude, emotions, words, and beliefs are bigger than you and will affect those around you in life and in business just like you learned from the game. Here's one account of how my legacy might read from a third-person perspective:

> **Derrick realizes his last name has become more important than his first—it's now his legacy.** He now has to start hustling for the sake of his last name. For this is the name his wife will have and the name his future child will bear. Derrick now knows that every choice he makes will affect those who bear his last name (that includes those who came before him and those who come after him). At this point Derrick realizes he will now have responsibilities as a man and husband; he must be the leader as well as the provider and supporter for his wife. He understands the marriage might get rocky; finances might be up and down; illness and employment might come and go; but regardless of what happens, he can't be quick to turn and run, fold up shop, tap out and quit if and when those times hit. This will be the fourth quarter when its fourth and goal at the goal line, only now the game is life, or business, and Furlow knows it will be up to him to make a play because his last name is depending on it.
>
> Furlow also realizes that someday, as a father, he must provide, protect, and guide his children as well as be the example of a godly man. When Derrick Furlow looks back, he will finally see what his parents meant when they told him it wasn't all about him. He will finally understand why his professors (and coaches) addressed him by his last name. He will understand why his teammates and coaches pushed him beyond exhaustion so he

could learn how to bend but not break, fight and run, endure and not quit when things were hard. He will finally see that once it was all said and done, everything had come full circle, it would be bigger than him, and that's what life had been telling him all along, but he didn't see the bigger picture for the longest time.

To this very day in my career, I work knowing that my job is bigger than me in terms of my decisions, deals, actions, videos, posts . . . whatever I do, I understand it's representing my last name. The decisions I make or do not make are attached to my last name. So if **I don't want a poor decision to outlive me, then I shouldn't make it.** Learning and respecting this bigger-than-me lesson wholeheartedly has helped steer me down a path of intentional and purposeful living, especially when it came to my career path. Whether it was from network marketing, sales, speaking, brokering deals, or writing this book, I knew the outcome was bigger than me, but I strive to leave my mark on the outcome by impacting, inspiring, and empowering everyone involved.

Whatever I do, I understand it's representing my last name, the decisions I make or do not make are attached to my last name. So if I don't want a poor decision to outlive me, then I shouldn't make it.

In my first sales job, I knew I had a product that could change people's lives, but early on relaying that message to prospective buyers wasn't as important to me as my commission check was. I soon realized that to be more successful in sales, I needed to stop focusing on my commissions and start telling customers what the product could do for them—that was bigger than me, and once I understood that, my commission checks went up.

You may be a brand (an entrepreneur), or have a company with employees or business partners, or you could even be an investor, or just a hardworking citizen. Whatever you are, please get this: **Everything that is happening to you is not happening just to you or just for you.** The outcome will always directly and indirectly affect those around you and those who come after you. Whatever you do or don't do, just know that it's bigger than you.

Sports, Life, Business Takeaways: Chapter 10

While reviewing the lessons presented in this chapter and summarized below, take the time to think about what early lessons, like the ones here, that you have learned in life that could benefit you in other areas. Write them down and jot down a few notes about how you can use them now, using the space to write at the end of the Takeaways.

1. **Who am I playing for?** Whether it's in the game of sports, life, or business, someone or something is depending on you: your spouse, your mom, your dad, yourself, your situation, your kids, your grandparents, your livelihood, God, your employer, an investor, your business partner . . . who or what is it? **Determining that answer is your first step to realizing that everything you do is for something bigger than you. Whether it's good, bad, ugly, sin related, or Savior related, it's bigger than you.**

2. **Honoring those who came before you and paving a way to leave a legacy for those coming after you.** That's one of the first things the game of football taught me: the more I learned, the more I realized that (the legacy factor) was a formula for life as well. **The older I got, the more this became important to me; it was a part of the wisdom I use to motivate me to get to where I am today, even as a work still in**

progress. Leaving a legacy for those coming after me is a driving force for me, and it should be for you as well. It's exciting for me to know that I get a chance to personally be responsible for making a difference for the advancement of family, friends, organizations, and mankind, just like others who did that came before me.

3. Adopt the concept of **doing what is best for the** *team*. **In life, away from sports, that refers to family; in business, it means partners. Now that I'm playing the game of life and business, I use this idea of** *team* **as I evaluate my next moves, because what's good for me might not be always good for the team, but what is good for the team might not always be good for me. This perspective might not dictate every outcome, but it does cut out the selfish thinking that can affect any of us when facing real life and big business decisions.**

4. **It is about you, but everything that you do will directly or indirectly affect someone around you at some point.** This is a fact of life served cold at times, and the faster we accept it, the better we can become because of it.

5. **By the time he got to college, Derrick (that's me) realized his last name (Furlow) had become more important than his first (the legacy thing).** Furlow now has to start hustling

for his last name. **When we get to this point, we truly understand what life is about. I must say, this normally doesn't happen until people experience real life—sometimes it's a wife; sometimes it's kids; sometimes it's the grand-kids. Now that you are aware of this—how your last name is now your brand for all the world to see—do not wait until it's too late to start building your legacy. Do this before you run out of time.**

6. Everything that is happening to you is not hap-pening **JUST TO YOU**, or **JUST FOR YOU**. It's **bigger than you.**

Chapter 10 Notes

_____

_____

_____

_____

_____

_____

_____

_____

_____

_____

_____

_____

_____

_____

SPORTS   **LIFE**   BUSINESS

11
CHAMPION'S MIND-SET

THE TRUE TEST DOESN'T START UNTIL LIFE AFTER SPORTS. **That's when you can look at yourself to see what you truly became through the process of playing sports.** When the game is over, you will have built your **integrity**, presumably, which will set the stage for how you will be viewed by friends, family, peers, business partners, and other people you will meet. You also will have had your **character** tested to see if you are true to who you are. Your sport was designed to create a mental, physical, emotional, spiritual champion, which is an uncommon breed. It's like you are a caterpillar and the process of the game is your cocoon before you are released like a butterfly into life and business. When your playing days are done, you will emerge from the cocoon as a butterfly, fully developed and ready to fly—ready to go after life and business with a plan; or you could come out the same way you went in; not ready and unsure of your future.

By making it this far into the book, you probably realize that for that type of development, it starts with a mind-set—

not just any type of mind-set, but a mind-set of a champion. A champion's mind-set is not just talk, it's the outlook you have after realizing how much sweat equity you have invested into whatever you have been doing. It's the intangibles that were created from the work you put in. Let's take that mind-set and apply it into every other phase of your life.

All the lessons I have shared with you that I learned from the game of football should have stirred up memories that you have and perhaps brought to mind lessons that your sport, your life, or your business has taught you. If so, that's great. If it hasn't, go back and read through the book, putting yourself into your own versions of the circumstances that I described. For those of you who have lessons you have learned but forgotten about, here is a missing piece: **application**—applying it to what comes next in your life. Only you know what that is: I can't do it for you.

The game was good to you, it ran its course, and it served its purpose for that season of your life. But the lessons you learned from the game will serve their purpose for the rest of your life, if you bother to apply them.

Once you remember what you are capable of and have reminded yourself of what your particular skill set is, and that you have achieved success before, you should be confident in knowing you are more than capable of doing it again in a different setting. This is the champion's mind-set. It's time for you to execute again, like you have in the past.

Every play you ever practiced and watched, it came down to executing the play when it counted. Wherever you are right now—in sports, life, or business—it comes down to execution. **The game was good to you, it ran its course, and it served its purpose for that season of your life. But the lessons you learned from the game will serve their purpose**

for the rest of your life, if you apply them. This is the **champion's mind-set.** You are unstoppable, you have been **knocked down** before mentally, but you persevered, got up, and kept going. You have been knocked down before physically, but that didn't stop you, either. Just think, that was all for a game, something you enjoyed. How much more can you endure if your way of life, spouse, kids, faith, health, or your business career, job, investment, invention, company are at stake?

When it comes down to mind-set, it is often a way of thinking on which we operate based on our upbringing, environment, and the people who have influenced us the most.

Your mind-set will often change as you grow up, and as you grow the factors that helped create your mind-set will often change as well. When you were younger, numerous factors would help determine, shape, mold, and grow your mind. Once you hit a certain point in life, the books you read and the people and things you listen to become more involved in shaping your mind-set. You must guard your mind, just like you guarded your game. In your game, it wasn't open practice every day; your coach didn't let just anybody coach you up and tell you about your game. Well the same rules apply, **Once you change the inside, you can change your outside.**

If you are not yet reading books and other publications to enrich your mind-set, start now. If you do not like the way your friends think, find new friends. If you don't like the direction your game is going, change it. These three factors will dominate how your mind-set is molded; this is critical for developing a "champion's mind-set." This champion's mind-set can be easily compared to the mind-set you had in that one particular area of your life where you knew you were the best. You remember that feeling, whether you had it as an adult or as a child, you can remember that mind-set of knowing you were the best. It was the confidence you exuded, the belief you had.

The **philosophy** you had had a part in creating the **attitude** you had about it. All this goes into determining the **actions** of having a champion's mind-set. That is the same mind-set that you must keep in life and in business. **The mind-set I had in sports when competing is the same one I have in life and in business.** Nothing has changed except the stage. Most athletes retire their mind-set once they leave their sport and then get into the game of life and business and wonder what happened. What happened to that edge, that spirit they had previously? They abandoned it; they failed to transition it to the rest of their lives

The champion's mind-set you had in sports—you neglected to plant and cultivate those seeds in other areas of your mind. Huge mistake. Once you left the game, you didn't take your champion's mind-set with you—it stayed behind with the game from which you departed. This is the biggest missing piece to the puzzle on why athletes struggle in the game of life and business after sports. It could be your **ego**—your wanting to still enjoy the athlete's lavish lifestyle without the willingness to accept the fact you were essentially starting over in a new world, with another ladder of success to climb. If, however, you had carried over the champion's mind-set after the game, you would retain the ability to go out and create a new lifestyle to stroke your ego. Or maybe you didn't make it to that next level in your sport but still hold on to that **"hoop dream,"** because you now feel like precious time has passed you by. This is what I say to you: You will be all right. Get over it, it happens. Life goes on. Now, reach back and grab that same burning desire you had for the game and apply it to something else. Bring it forward.

Finally, you could be one of those who **"get it,"** meaning you played your game and gave it all that you had to give. In return, you took away so much from the game, that whether you played on the next level or not, you'd be **intangibly rich forever**. You knew what you have learned and can go apply that knowledge to any area outside sports and create success, which is the ultimate prize. So just remember throughout your journey that the game is a small part of the big picture; it only looks big at the time because that is all that you see. But the lessons it will teach you will be lessons that create the champion's mind-set, which you can apply to the big picture once the game is over.

From this point forward, once you think of the champion's mind-set, look back at your resume of successes, lessons, and principles used to help you create that success. Focus on what you used and how you used it to create that success. Then imagine that feeling you had during that moment. That's what this book will create for you if you apply the principles and lessons featured in each chapter. It will give you the ability to cultivate and use the champion's mind-set that the game created in you, that perhaps you forgot you had or just did not know how to tap into it.

Sports, Life, Business Takeaways: Chapter 11

While reviewing the lessons presented in this chapter and summarized below, take the time to think about what early lessons, like the ones here, that you have learned in life that could benefit you in other areas. Write them down and jot down a few notes about how you can use them now, using the space to write at the end of the Takeaways.

1. **The true test does not start until life after sports. That's when you can look at yourself to see what you became throughout your process of playing the game.** This is when you find out if you were just in the game or if the game is in you. Hopefully, it is both. If so, your next phase of life or business will be prosperous because you are aware of what it takes; you will possess the mind-set and will have applied it before. Now all you must do is reapply that mind-set in a different phase.

2. By the time you have finished playing the game, you will have built your **integrity, presumably. That will set the stage for who you are and what you stand for as a person. This will go a long way in determining how you feel about yourself and how others feel about you in life or business. Not only will the game build your integrity for you, it will also test it.**

3. Your **character** was tested to see if you are true to who you are. **The game builds and tests integrity and character, just like car manufacturers build and test cars using crash dummies. They want to make sure the car is road worthy, because once the car has left the factory and is on the road, it is real life. There is nothing the car builder can do; the car must be able to endure in the real world. That's exactly what the game does for athletes; however, most never take the crash test seriously until they are out in the real world and it is too late.**

4. **Application.** Now that you remember what you are capable of and that you have achieved prior success, just **repeat those same principles and actions.**

5. **The game was good to you. It ran its course, and it served its purpose for that season of your life. But the lessons you learned from the game will serve their purpose for the rest of your life.** Realize that the game is only a small part of your life, even though it seems so big while going through it. It seems bigger than it is because that's all you know. Just rest assured that there is more to life than the game. Once you are done, you will realize that the game gave you one way to fulfill your purpose, but there are a million more ways to fulfill it that work

just as well. Just apply the old principles that worked to whatever your new game is.

6. The **philosophy** you have creates the **attitude** you have about anything and everything. All this together demonstrates the **actions** of having a champion's mind-set. **There is no way around these. Either you will use them to help you create the champion's mind-set that gets you ahead in life and business, or you get the wrong mind-set, which will move you backward.**

7. **Be intangibly rich forever** because you knew from what you had learned that you could go apply that knowledge to any area outside sports and create success, which is the ultimate prize.

SPORTS   LIFE   BUSINESS

EPILOGUE

NOW THAT YOU HAVE CONCLUDED *What's Next? (SLB) Sports Life Business: How to Transition Like a Champion*, I hope you feel encouraged and inspired. More importantly, I hope you are now educated on what the game can teach you—if you don't miss the message. When you put down this book, I hope you decide to choose an excuse to win and then get to work. Know that your time is coming. To get to the next level in your sport, your life, or your business, you might have to take the stairs. So be it. The principles covered in this book can turn those stairs into a fast-moving escalator if you allow them to. Always remember your advantage is your past; however good, bad, or ugly it might have looked at the time, this is where your lessons reside. When it came to the game you played, remember that "You can't start it over, but you can finish it strong." Regardless where you are in life now, I challenge you to finish it strong.

On the following page are a few maxims I've pulled together to help you put your own pieces of the puzzle together:

- You have to examine you.
- You can't look good and be uncomfortable at the same time.
- What are you doing daily?
- Things worth doing are worth doing every day.
- Practice your craft and hone your skills.
- Do the things that no one sees.
- Your decisions determine everything.
- Instead of being a want-to-be, become a work-to-be. Work to become all the things you want to be.
- There are two ways you can learn: Learn knowledge by studying. Learn action by taking action.
- Never postpone anything you can do now.
- The only person who can make your life work out is you. Be responsible for your life.
- You must stay grounded enough to remember your past but hungry enough to relentlessly work on your future.
- Everything you have succeeded at in life, you were only competing against one thing—your doubts.
- We want it all right now and often forget that most things worth having come in delayed gratification. Make sure you are prepared to receive it.

SPORTS   LIFE   BUSINESS

ABOUT THE AUTHOR

DERRICK FURLOW, JR. PLAYED FOOTBALL AT THE UNIVERSITY OF TENNESSEE. While doing so, he completed his bachelor's and master's degrees. He is an entrepreneur at heart, speaker, author, and servant to his community. He believes sports are a direct correlation to life and teaches clients everything they need to know to be successful in life and business. He created a place where they all came together in the form of his "Sports Life Business" program for the sole purpose of setting a new standard for how athletes and people transition from one phase of their life to the next! He is living out his purpose here on earth to Impact, inspire, and empower people while setting the new standard for transitioning.